Going for the Blue

ROGER A. CARAS

GOING
FOR THE
BLUE

Inside the World
of Show Dogs and
Dog Shows

WARNER BOOKS

A Time Warner Company

Warner Books, Inc., 1271 Avenue of the Americas, New York, NY 10020

Visit our Web site at www.twbookmark.com

 A Time Warner Company

Printed in the United States of America

First Printing: February 2001

10 9 8 7 6 5 4 3 2 1

Library of Congress Cataloging-in-Publication Data
Caras, Roger A.
    Going for the blue : inside the world of show dogs and dog shows / by Roger A. Caras.
        p. cm.
    ISBN 0-446-52644-4
    1. Dog shows. 2. Show dogs. 3. Dog shows—United States. 4. Show dogs—United
States. I. Title.

SF425 .C37 2001
636.7'0811—dc21   00-063398

To my wife, Jill, and our kids, Pamela and Clay—and theirs, Sarah, Joshua, Abaigeal, and Hannah—and Joe and Sheila, son- and daughter-in-law (we couldn't have done better if we had picked them ourselves), this book is dedicated. Ours is an expansive clan of dog lovers. We have sixteen canine objects of our affection among us at the moment. (And a parcel of cats and horses, too.) It's a good start.

Acknowledgments

A great many people have contributed to this book simply by talking to me and letting me see and feel their enthusiasm. I am grateful to each of them, all of them, although the list is too long to spell out here. I have spent my life surrounded by such people. And their dogs! They have all been my teachers.

Our dogs here on Thistle Hill Farm are, in no particular order, the Greyhounds, Sirius (or Xyerius), Jon-Jon, Lilly, and Hyacinth; the Basset, Pearl; the Yorkie, Sam; the Whippet, Topi; the Jack Russell Terriers, Olivia and Maude; and the West Highland White Terriers, Angus and MacGregor. They are all different, each special, without exception, and they offer an incredible amount of love.

And very special thanks to Robert Taylor and Rhonda Kumm for reading the manuscript and saving me from myself.

Contents

Introduction

This book is about dog shows, how they work, what they mean, and how they reflect an incredibly complex relationship, one that has grown to embrace two very different species of mammals. That relationship has taken thousands of years to develop and a veritable eternity of evolution.

But before there can be a dog show, the players have to exist and be in place: the dogs and us and, of course, underlying it all, our wonderful relationship. No question, though, there have to be dogs. All breeds of domestic dogs we know from around the world belong to just one species: *Canis familiaris*. But their diversity is incredible. A touch of the history of that species, then, but just a touch, will do.

Conventional wisdom, for whatever it might be worth, has caveman (more likely cavewoman, say I) extracting the first or at least the earliest known dogs from the loins of wolves somewhere between fifteen and twenty thousand years ago. Think of them as "dawn dogs" intent upon changing our world for us (and they did). Think of them as well as future works of art and important factors in our health and well-being. The place where the linkup first began to appear has never been identified with certainty, although it has been pondered and discussed endlessly. There are more experts on this subject than there are on how to play golf or how to make chili. One of the places that has been suggested is the Middle East, between what are now Israel and India. In this scenario, the ancestral beast is said to have been a small subspecies of wolf, *Canis lupus pallipes,* a form that is still found in many parts of that mostly arid region. They are rather small—coyote size—and, as I can attest, noisy at night. When the moon slides across the blue-gray early-night sky of the desert, as the sky itself turns into black velvet flecked with a billion times a billion stars, out beyond the palm trees that stand now in silhouette, the little wolf, accused ancestor of all the dogs we know, sings mournfully in a language we can't understand but in a mood we do understand all too well, as do the sheep and goats that the wolves covet and stalk. Modern domestic dogs, sleeping outside the tents in the oasis, lift their heads and answer in their modified voices. Do they understand each other, these dogs and their ancestors? In some ways they must. They come from the same limb of the same tree in the same corner of the garden.

It is at least possible (not certain, surely, but possible) that the cave dwellers who made this first connection with our dog ancestors were not even of our species or at least of our exact kind. Perhaps they were Cro-Magnon people, probably, in part, exterminators of earlier Neanderthal man and the precursors of *Homo sapiens*—us, in other words, or modern man. If some of the extraordinary ages that have been suggested for the emergence of domestic dogs are even half true, the first dog trainers would have to have been other than our kind. (*Man*, or *he*, as used in this book, does not imply gender but entire species. All of the he/she, him/her constructions I have ever tried to use ultimately seemed flat, silly, and self-conscious. They would serve no useful purpose here. Let it be said that in many areas of cultural progress [agriculture, for example, at least in some cultures] women were the leading lights. An interesting idea: "Old Lady McDonald had a farm . . ." Since we can't be sure in most cases of the relative participation of the genders in the inventiveness of our species, we will let it rest. *Man*, as we use it here, is *man* and *woman*, with no prejudice intended.)

Our relationship with our dogs today is probably far different from the form it took in the cave. Such things as style and aesthetics would not have been very important considerations back then. Little or no energy was spent on cosmetic touches until quite recently. We can surmise that the cuddle factor was less apparent, but the difference was more on the human's part than on the dog's. It seems fairly certain that cave or dawn dogs, fresh out of their ancestral wolves' genes, liked being scratched and petted just as dogs do today. Wolves raised as supposed pets today and intensely socialized do their best to encourage comfort giving; they are as hedonistic as dogs are. (Wolves, however, are not dogs and they can be bad for your health. They are not recommended as family pets under any circumstances. Part wolves, wolf-dog hybrids, whatever the wolf content of their genes, are, if anything, worse. The dog in them has taken away their natural fear of man. That is not good. It can be lethal or at least disfiguring.)

It has been known for a long time that pet owners who scratch, stroke, or in any way pat their companions have lower blood pressure and a slower heart rate while they are so engaged. That tends toward longer life and the appearance of children who are likely to be pet lovers, too. Our pets are good for us. In a sense, they have selectively bred us. I think our collective ego should be able to handle that.

Very recent studies involved putting heart monitors on dogs. As might be expected, the offer of either food or play cause a marked increase in heartbeats per minute. When the dogs were petted in any of the usual ways, however, their heart rate dropped and the animals "cooled out." We are good for our pets. There has been at the very least fifteen to twenty thousand years of reciprocity. Neither man nor dog should be alone. We are both pack animals, and, it seems, we were made for each other.

What this means is that for 150 centuries or more (how much more we may be slow in learning), men and dogs have mutually enjoyed the sense of touch. It has been good for both of us, and in terms of life span, dog-loving people and people-focused dogs tend to live longer and create more of their own kind. This hasn't been by accident; it has been part of the evolution of both species. It is an integral part of our bond.

Dogs, almost from the beginning, began splitting off into new breeds, none of which from those earliest years are known now. Just as with so many wild species, dog breeds have become extinct and been replaced by the natural forces of evolution at work. We think we know some basic breeds from seven to nine thousand years ago—the Ibizan Hound, Saluki, and Samoyed are possible examples—but we can't speak with confidence of anything much earlier than that.

A word on the science of it all. When animals are held in captivity and isolated from the wild population of their species, they will continue to mate, becoming more inbred with each generation. They become, as a group, what is known as a deme. A phenomenon known as genetic drift comes into play as the captive animals evolve through the same process of natural selection as any population of their species. But in this case it responds to the opportunities and challenges of the new environment provided by human beings. Whether we're aware of it or not at the time, we play a vital role. That is generally true of all of our domestic animals, about forty-five of them. We create the habitat and provide them with nutrition (or neglect), as well as frequently creating rigidly controlled mating opportunities. In the case of purebred dogs, we guard that charge jealously. We are the ultimate matchmakers.

How did early man or preman—Neanderthal, Cro-Magnon, or modern—know the secret of selective breeding? It is unlikely that cave dwellers 150 centuries ago understood the calendar, the sociology, the chemistry, and the mechanics of their own sexuality. Sex then was surely essentially opportunistic, often involving migrants who might never come that way again. Today we would think of much of what happened in and around the cave as rape. Sometimes, three-quarters of a year later, there would be a baby. Most of the time there would not, for a whole host of reasons. In that kind of hit-and-miss, touch-and-go world, an understandable connection between act and result was hard to make.

With no knowledge of genetics then, how did cave-living dog fanciers plan selective breeding? They couldn't—it had to have come from influences far beyond their imagination or capacity to wonder. Serendipity played a major role. There were a lot of *oops* and *wows* in procreation eons before genes and the elusive DNA were unmasked.

No animal we know of was domesticated by early man unless that animal was already locked into a relationship with man. There had to be a link, and it took the form of hunting. Man hunted many species for meat and pelts—almost everything around him, in fact, and the wolf was on the hit list. If a band of hunters whooping, hollering, and brandishing flaming torches and throwing rocks neutralized a pair of adult wolves, they frequently ended up with a litter of cubs to show for their efforts. Without refrigeration they learned soon enough not to kill more cubs than they could eat right away, or the surplus would become rancid and make them ill. Dead and rotting meat could make even a cave dwelling far worse than it had to be. A better idea was to keep the cubs alive in a corner of the cave until they were needed for the pot. (Actually, Paleolithic man and his precursors didn't have pottery. Sad to contemplate, but those first evolving dog fanciers probably roasted wolf cubs the way we do marshmallows.)

Since humans are born quite thoroughly helpless, we have a years-long tutorial period. To accommodate this species characteristic, our mothers fulfill the nurturing role. Given a nurturing mother with or without her own baby in hand, add a litter of squirming and squealing wolf babies, all of which display endearing characteristics, and we were on our way to dogdom. That route, given the human capacity for pride and competitiveness, led inexorably to formalized dog shows in England in the middle of the nineteenth century. It was slow in coming but it was foreordained.

The first endearing characteristic that caveman serendipitously selected for was gentleness. The roughnecks, the biters in the crowd, were undoubtedly the first onto the barbecue. It was perfectly natural to opt for easy keepers, and early man almost surely did exactly that, although ignorant of the significance of what he was doing. If a dweller in cave A had a male easy keeper and the folks in cave B had a female with the same kind of disposition, the stage was set. The cubs grew, they interacted as juveniles, they mated, and a breed characteristic—relative gentleness—was intensified dog generation by dog generation. With gestation a brief sixty-three days and sexual maturity under a year, things would have moved along smartly. It is interesting that we still look for that in our dogs today, a certain softness.

It is a fair assumption that cave people had totems in the fabric of their beliefs. Perhaps it was a white wolf, a black one, or a yellow one, but it is likely that one form or another was considered sacred in some primitive way. They couldn't be killed without taking great risks with the powerful ones who lived in the mists on the mountain or in the face of the storm. If cave families A and B both had gentler-than-usual maturing wolves of the same color, those wolves would eventually have the opportunity to mate, and breed differentiation would be unavoidable within the deme over time. Time was one thing there was plenty of, time and the incredible elasticity of the wolf-dog gene.

As noted, all dogs belong to the same species (*Canis familiaris*) no matter what their breed. The wolf-dog gene package has proven to be remarkably flexible, capable of startling diversity and adjustment. Consider this logical comparison: All domestic cat breeds, descendants of the North African wildcat, also belong to a single species, *Felis catus*. Excepting the occasional obese individual, our domestic cats generally weigh between eight and twenty pounds, that is, the largest normal cat weighs two and one-half times as much as the smallest normal cat. Among dogs the case is amazingly different. A Saint Bernard or a New-foundland can weigh some thirty-three times as much as a fully mature Chihuahua. That is flexibility! In fact, it is awe-some. If we had a two-hundred-pound Siamese cat we would need a backhoe to handle the litter box and Valium for ourselves. Such cats would make nervous wrecks of our canaries, not to mention the local mice. Only at battalion strength could our dogs worry such cats. Which cushion in the sun could such a cat claim? Every one in the house.

What do we know of the first breeds? There were Greyhound-like dogs in the Middle East and Mastiff-like dogs in Tibet. We speak of both the Greyhound and the Mastiff today as foundation breeds. Indeed, they are. There were also lap dogs and what were apparently herding dogs. The very early dates we hear postulated wouldn't apply to herding dogs. There was nothing for them to herd until roughly fifteen thousand years ago, where most students still date dog emergence, close to the domestication of goats, sheep, and reindeer. And so the mystery goes on. How did dogs get to Tibet to become Mastiff-like, from whence they came back to fight as gladiators in Rome and then helped the legions invade central Europe and the British Isles as war dogs? (When the Romans got to the British Isles with their Mastiffs, they found the inhabitants there already had a Mastiff of their own. That latter dog is the ancestor of our Mastiffs today. The Roman dogs we refer to as Neopolitan

Mastiffs, or Neos, and they are not recognized by the American Kennel Club.)

The early distinguishable breeds were essentially utilitarian except for the lap dogs—which were that as well, but in a special way. Dogs were tools. In time of famine, evolving dogs (unlike totemic or preferentially colored wolves) could be eaten. They were also noisy and territorial when gigantic cave bears, lions, or strange people from another valley approached the stronghold. They could assist in hunting because wolves are natural herders and pack workers just as human beings are. If you question whether the wolf's herding instinct came down through time to reside in our dogs today, watch Border Collies at work. You are seeing controlled aggression coupled with amazing intelligence perform near-miracles of cooperation.

So there we have the pattern and the path. By ten thousand years ago true dogs had evolved that could assume any utilitarian role we can imagine, although, presumably, aesthetics was not yet a factor. Of course, none of us has lived a caveman's life, with its ancient imperatives, and there could be elements to the dog-man equation we simply haven't guessed at. What we do know is that in the nineteenth century a beauty contest was launched in many breeds, without any diminution of utilitarian concerns.

Some dogs were singled out for one job only, companionship. The Toy Group (we will be getting to the groups in the chapters ahead) is made up of what are essentially miniaturized dogs whose task is both emotional and aesthetic. They are joy givers as companions. Dogs like the Miniature Pinscher, the Yorkshire Terrier, the Pug, and the Maltese have few other assignments now besides getting and giving love. It is interesting that despite the fact that we know so little about very early men and women as individuals, we do know that way back at some phase of the Stone Age they had lap dogs. Without this one clue we would be loath to think of a hairy-shouldered, club-swinging caveman as a sentimental snuggler. Some lap dogs, we can suppose, were snacks, but somehow I think not all, except in that, as today, they fed their owners' souls.

In the seemingly hodgepodge miscellany called the Nonsporting Group, breeds like the Standard and Miniature Poodles, French Bulldog, Dalmatian, Chow Chow, and Boston Terrier are short on anything other than emotional and aesthetic assignments. That is not true of Border Collies, Labrador Retrievers, Australian Cattle Dogs, and many other guard, farm, and field dogs. In a good many places they work for a living, but still, in our time they are also expected to attain a high level of beauty in their conformation. Just when beauty became important and why it began to matter is probably a whole aspect of our own evolution that we cannot readily decipher. The dogs were our canvases with their incredibly malleable genes, but we were and still are the artists.

Today man's concern with dogs is very different from what it was long ago. We are, after all, not talking about the Neolithic, the New Stone Age—or even the Mesolithic, the Middle Stone Age—but the Paleolithic, the *Old* Stone Age. From then till now many facets of our relationship with dogs have changed.

But, then, what hasn't?

What Is a Show Dog Supposed to Look Like?

Chapter

1

There are estimated to be more than twenty million pure-bred dogs in the United States today. Not 10 percent of these dogs are likely to see the inside of a show ring. And relatively few of those that are launched by novice and perhaps overexcited owners will stay there for very long. In most cases one of two things will happen. Either it will quickly become apparent that the dog (technically *dog* refers only to the male, but the term will be used generically hereafter, with a few exceptions) or bitch (female—and they don't call them that for nothing!) does not stand a chance against the really heavy hitters that are lying in wait for someone with the temerity to challenge them, or the time and cost of continuing or finishing will prove prohibitive. (Finishing means getting a championship. In an average year the AKC—American Kennel Club—records close to twenty-one thousand new champions, dogs that have earned enough points to finish.)

Stardom is a lovely concept and an intriguing goal, but it can be a costly state to achieve. It is possible—a little unusual but possible—to end up with a six-figure tab for just one year of showing, or campaigning, as the search for stardom is generally called. Add to that the time and the wear and tear of travel on your dog and yourself and you are into one heavy-duty hobby. This is industrial-weight "fun." The next steps up from there in the costly Fun department could be a private jet (crew or owner driven) or perhaps a sports franchise or, of course, a stable full of Thoroughbreds. Still, the dog thing can be done for less, indeed a lot less if that is the goal. Surprisingly, a great many thousands of people show their dogs to their own satisfaction for a fraction of that six-figure cost. However, campaigning is never really cheap, and eventually, if you have the right dog and you are stubborn enough, you may have to dig in and pay out a great deal of money to realize your goals for your dog—who may love the whole showing gig but does not have goals or ambitions himself.

What Is a Purebred Dog?

A purebred dog, very simply, is a member of a breed recognized by the AKC that has achieved a high degree of genetic stability. There are many dogs of this description that are recognized as breeds in other countries but not in the United States. When two dogs of one breed are given an opportunity to mate, the puppies that result will look reasonably like their parents and each other. That, certainly, is the plan. And that reasonable level of predictability is terribly important to some people, whether or not they are going to show their very good friend. There are standards for each breed (we will be getting to them soon enough), and those puppies between sixteen and roughly fifty-two weeks of age that appear to be up to the standard, or at least close to it, can be considered at least potential show dogs. It is a matter of opinion. Those who fall very far short are considered pet-quality purebred dogs. They can make wonderful pets, they can give and get love along with the best of them, and, in fact, they may still be very handsome animals. It is just that somehow they don't conform or aren't close enough to the way the standard says they have to look. The shortfall in majestic good looks or movement may not even be discernible to the layman. The glitch can be so arcane that only breeders, handlers, and judges can pick up on it.

Standards are unforgiving. A dog may be superb at aiding the physically impaired, or fantastic at rescue work or in detecting guns, bombs, and drugs in luggage, but if it misses meeting the standards by even just a little, it will have no hope in the ring. There are just too many dogs out there that don't miss the standards to offer the wanna-be much hope for time in the spotlight. If you are a dog lover, this really should not matter—loving, after all, is loving. Show-quality purebred dogs are no better for hugging and tennis-ball chasing than pet-quality purebreds—or random-breds, for that matter.

To indicate how unforgiving the standards can be, I'll

give you some examples of the kinds of things that can go wrong, according to the official published AKC standards. These are only the briefest samples.

They say that no one is perfect, and so it is with dogs. Each breed has some potential flaws. They are designated as faults in the standard, and rarely is this beauty test very much easier for one breed with its potential faults than for another. The Soft-Coated Wheaten Terrier (Terrier Group), for example, must have a nose that is uniformly black and large for the size of the dog. The eyes must be hazel or brown and have black rims. They had better be. The judges know all these things, and they will be looking. (When it comes to dog-show judges, by the way, "he" is just as likely to be "she." That is also true for handlers.)

The Bulldog (Nonsporting Group) is often erroneously, but without evil intent, referred to as the English Bulldog. There is no such breed. The Bulldog's standard says his coat must be straight, short, flat, close, of fine texture, smooth, and glossy with no fringe, feather, or curl. I love my kids and grandchildren and they are all beautiful and brilliant (of course), but they couldn't pass such a stringent test of consistency! The rest of the Bulldog standard reveals that its coat is the easiest of the hurdles it has to clear. I love Bulldogs, but God love them, a Bulldog is an ambulatory bundle of improbabilities.

The Akita (Working Group) must have lips that are black and not pendulous; the tongue is pink. The tail is large and full, set high and carried over the back or against the flank in a three-quarter, full, or double curl, always dipping to or below the level of the back. On a three-quarter curl the tip droops well down the flank. The root is large and strong, as is the dog itself. The tailbone reaches the hock when it is let down. The hair on the tail must be coarse, straight, and full, with no appearance of a plume.

The Afghan Hound (Hound Group), according to the standards, has eyes that are almond shaped (almost triangular) and never full or bulgy, and they must be dark in color. The ears are long and are set approximately on the level of the outer corners of the eyes. The leather (the meaty, flesh-and-cartilage part of the ear) reaches nearly to the end of the dog's nose and is covered with long silky hair. The stipulation that the ears reach *nearly* to the end of the dog's nose does give the judge a little wiggle room, room for interpretation. What, after all, does *nearly* mean? It is a judgment call, and that is what judges do: they pass judgment. One judge's "nearly" is another judge's clean miss. Any memorialized latitude like that could lay the groundwork for politics and favoritism. *Could* doesn't mean *does*, but the opportunity is there and so is the history.

. . . AND NOT SO PURE

In this book we talk a good deal about breeding and puppies, yet we live in this tragic throw-away society where every year dogs (and cats) by the millions are put to sleep because there aren't enough good homes for them. Why breed more?

7

First of all, no pet-quality dog (or cat), purebred or random-bred, should ever be allowed to reproduce. There is no rational argument for breeding dogs whose genes are not needed to improve the genetic package of its breed. On the other hand, bear in mind that a dog that has been spayed or neutered can't show in conformation, so neutering is a serious, permanent decision. There is no going back. The show-quality dogs we are talking about here don't end up on the surplus rolls. People are waiting in line for them. If those people want a show dog or just a pet dog of a specific breed, it is a personal choice accomplished with their own discretionary funds. In shelters across the country, the number of purebred dogs runs only 18 to 20 percent of the total shelter-dog population. The other dogs are random-bred and can make super pets—all dogs are potentially outstanding companions whether purebred or not.

The purebred dogs found in shelters rarely come from the kind of kennels we will be talking about. It's more likely they were purchased at an exorbitant price in a pet shop (which usually charges much more than a top kennel would), which in turn bought them from a middleman who got them from a puppy mill. The whole business is both sordid and profitable. This mass production of dogs is nevertheless licensed by the federal government, with a sanction from the AKC. All these puppies, however badly off they may be, still get AKC papers.

Puppy mills are an evil, ugly concept. It is mass breeding without regard for bloodlines and with the dogs usually terribly mistreated. It is difficult to imagine how bad they are until you have seen some. I have personally inspected scores of them and have never encountered one with so much as a single redeeming quality. They are concentration camps for ill, undersocialized puppies often set to be shipped weeks before it is even legal to do so. Typically the dogs from puppy mills and hence pet shops are sickly, and they must have thousands of dollars spent on them before they have even the slightest chance of being healthy. I can't say it has never happened, but a pet shop–puppy mill dog making it in any show or other form of competition is an extraordinarily rare event. They are the surplus purebred dogs we encounter in municipal control facilities or humane shelters and they deserve all the help and support we can give them. They are, however, not the show dogs we are contemplating here and should never be allowed to reproduce. The point can't be stressed often enough. However splendid a dog—any dog— may be, the idea is not to propagate genetic disasters. Dog shows have exactly the opposite goal.

EARLY HISTORY

Some further thoughts on a historical perspective. We should at least try to get these things in order.

If the dog was first developed and started on its way toward breed differentiation even as recently as fifteen thousand years ago, around thirteen thousand B.C., and Christopher Columbus didn't set sail for the New World until high tide on Friday afternoon, August 3, 1492, how is it that dogs were given ritual burials in areas that are now Idaho and Nantucket Island, eight thousand and four thousand years ago, respectively? How did dogs make incredible journeys millennia before Europeans? Almost certainly they didn't. It is a long walk (and a daunting swim) from Babylon to Boston. Consider some of the moves that would have to have been made if the "Middle East–little wolf only" scenario is accepted: from thence east to Tibet; then to somewhere in the South Pacific to link up with primitive navigators about to invade Australia, bringing their dogs (dingoes) with them (I have seen pariah-type dogs in the longhouses of mountainous areas of Borneo that matched the pariah dogs of Africa and mainland Asia). To North America eight thousand years ago, a site in Idaho called Jaguar Cave, where ritual burials took place, and then three or four thousand years later off the coast of what is now Massachusetts. To Peru, the high Andes, to live and evolve among the Inca; to central Mexico to live and evolve among the Aztec, Quantapec, and Toltec and their kin, and south of there to live and evolve among the Mayan peoples; with the Plains Indians in North America. In northern Japan; possibly in the New Guinea Highlands; and in areas of Africa not identified because they accompanied that vast continent's nomadic tribes and were probably used as trade goods.

One way or another, dogs got to those places, and in each and every one of them evolved according to the opportunities man provided. Our knowledge of all this is a patchwork of truths—we think—and not just a few maybes. In fact, we don't know much about this part of it at all. It is highly probable that dogs were on their way toward becoming hundreds of different breeds, perhaps thousands, in a great many parts of the world within the same time period, give or take a couple thousand years. No one kept a log or a studbook. There was no PKC—Paleolithic Kennel Club.

From time to time a venerable and distinguished scientist has come forth with the theory that the pretty little golden jackal (*Canis aureus*) of the African savanna was as ancestral to our dog as the wolf is or even more directly. No one seems to hold on to that theory for long. Typically, the distinguished and venerable scientist eventually apologizes and goes back to the wolf theory with something akin to his tail between his legs. I must say that the few times I have encountered the golden jackal in the wild and have been looked in the eye by them, there was the feeling of dog about them. Steady and intelligent, they pad off at a slow and deliberate trot into deeper grass. Wolves are somewhat like that, too, although they have the added dimension of their pack behavior, their social interactions.

By way of keeping our perspective and perhaps thoroughly confusing just about everybody: there are claims for true dog remains in North Africa 80,000 years ago (almost impossible to believe); in Europe, generally 17,000 years ago (that would be at least possible in the context of the Middle East claim of 15,000 years ago); in England, 7,500 years ago (that would be OK); in Zhoukoudian, China, 30,000 years ago (another tough one to imagine). Berber nomads are said to have had an active traffic in dogs 10,000 years ago, including Greyhound, Basenji, and small guard and herding dogs (again, OK); France, it has been suggested, 150,000 years ago (about ten times the conventional Middle East figure—well before there were *Homo sapiens*); Kent, England, 400,000 years ago! That last figure, for Kent, is almost certainly one of two things, fiction or fascinating error. When this symbiosis between man and dog really did get under way remains a matter of best guess. We do know that by four thousand years ago Greyhound-type and Mastiff-type dogs were established, as well as guard types other than Mastiffs, Sheepdogs, and, surprisingly, lap dogs.

Dogs, almost from the beginning, began splitting off into new breeds, of which we know none from the very early years. Just as with so many wild animal species, dog breeds have become extinct, being replaced by the natural forces of evolution. We think we know some basic breeds from seven to ten thousand years ago—the Ibizan Hound, the Saluki, and the Samoyed are possible examples—but nothing very much earlier than that can be spoken of with confidence.

WRIT IN BLACK AND WHITE

Many standards leave room for interpretation. For example, in the AKC standard for the Pointer we find: "The skull is of medium width approximately as wide as the length of the muzzle." Again, *approximately* leaves room for opinion rather than precision. There is no way of excising opinion and taste from dog-show judging any more than from an art competition or a chili cook-off. Nor would it necessarily be a good thing to do so, to stymie evolution by muffling the opinions of knowledgeable dog people.

Over the years, purebred dogs have changed, some breeds far more than others. In no small way those changes, constituting a form of evolution, have been the result of opinions and aesthetics. No dog standard is carved in stone. It is just a matter of taste, and although it can hang around for a long time, it is subject to evolution born of human judgment—or, or course, misjudgment. An outstanding show dog is a living, breathing wonder, and which dog is best and should be used to carry forward its breed's genes has to be decided, ultimately, by very doggy people: judges, breeders, and handlers. The dogs are usually willing and able. In real life, one dog doesn't look good to another in terms of a printed standard. But they sure can smell nice.

Many standards encourage judges to use their own judgment, the decision thereby gaining the value of their individual experience. In the AKC standard for the English Springer Spaniel we find this mandate: "The head is impressive without being heavy. Its beauty lies in the combination of strength and refinement. It is important that the size and proportion be in balance with the rest of the dog. Viewed in profile, the head should appear approximately the same length as the neck and should blend with the body and substance." This leaves a lot of room for opinion!

And even more room in the standard for the Great

How Tall Can They Be?
The Standards Speak

The standards hold height measured at the withers (shoulders) to be very important. Dogs that are too short or significantly outsized can be heavily faulted or, in many cases, disqualified and dismissed. Here are some size examples, from the largest to the smallest. All figures are in inches, dogs in the second column and bitches in the third. In some breeds there is significant sexual dimorphism (differences in form between sexes), and in other breeds there are no differences and the numbers specified in the standards overlap. In the tiny breeds, weight is more often given than height. (These are American Kennel Club requirements and may be inapplicable in the United Kingdom, for instance.)

BREED	DOGS	BITCHES
Great Dane	32+	28–30+
Irish Wolfhound	32	30
Scottish Deerhound	30–32+	28+
Mastiff	30+	27½+
Borzoi (Russian Wolfhound)	28	26
Newfoundland	28	26
Great Pyrenees	27–32	25–29
Saint Bernard	27½+	25½+
Irish Setter	27	25
Akita	26–28	24–26
Bloodhound	25–27	23–25

BREED	DOGS	BITCHES
Weimaraner	25–27	23–25
German Shepherd	24–26	22–24
Rottweiler	$23^3/_4$–27	$21^3/_4$–$25^3/_4$
Bernese Mountain Dog	23–$27^1/_2$	21–26
Golden Retriever	23–24	$21^1/_2$–$22^1/_2$
Boxer	$22^1/_2$–25	21–$23^1/_2$
Labrador Retriever	$22^1/_2$–$24^1/_2$	$21^1/_2$–$23^1/_2$
Whippet	19–22	18–21
Pug (largest of all the Toy breeds)	14–18	14–18
Italian Greyhound	13–15	13–15
Affenpinscher	$10^1/_4$	$10^1/_4$
Miniature Pinscher	10	$12^1/_2$
Papillon	8–11	8–11
Shih Tzu	8–11	8–11

Dane. It is described by the AKC as "of great size, powerful, well-balanced, elegant, dignified, courageous, friendly." That is not just a standard, it is an ode. That big guy sounds like someone I would like to know and sculpt.

A standard today is worth one hundred points in the ring if perfectly met (these points have nothing to do with standard points). Every dog and handler who enters the ring does so with the intention of convincing a judge that he or she has cast eyes on a rare one hundred–point dog. The judge frequently disagrees but is, I am sure, grateful for the opportunity.

Color can be an important aspect of standards. There are many breeds that we generally think of as pure black—at least, most people seem to see them that way. They are certain that a solid black coat has been mandated by the standards. In many breeds, black is just one of several solid colors allowed. The Newfoundland (usually but not inevitably black) and the extremely popular Labrador Retriever are examples. Others are the Pointer (albeit rare as solid black), Curly-Coated Retriever, Flat-Coated Retriever, Cocker Spaniel (one of the legitimate varieties of the Cocker Spaniel for show purposes is ASCOB, "any solid color other than black"). Included as well are the Field Spaniel, Afghan Hound, Basenji, Irish Wolfhound, Bearded Collie, Belgian Sheepdog, Bouvier des Flandres, Briard, Schnauzer (Giant, Standard, and Miniature), Great Dane, Puli, Scottish Terrier, Affenpinscher, Brussels Griffon, Pekingese, Pomeranian, Poodles (Toy, Miniature, and Standard), Pug, Chow Chow, and Schipperke. In the black version of some breeds, solid black (known as a self-color: all one color but with some lighter shadings allowed—indeed, expected) is mandated, but allowances are made for slight deviations. Only one breed standard is rigid when it states that solid black is an essential point on the way to perfection. Under the heading Disqualification, the first of three devilments listed for this breed is "any color other than solid black." And that breed, the AKC's only truly, unwaveringly black dog, is the little Dutch and Belgian barge watchdog, the Schipperke. A black Labrador may have a small white spot or mark on the chest and, like other breeds, may have a few white or gray hairs between the toes, the fewer the better. But not the Little Skipper, the diminutive version of a black Sheepdog from the Flemish provinces of Belgium. (Terrific dog, by the way, very long-lived.)

The whole matter of color can be confusing to newcomers, and it is a good plan to keep a book of standards close at hand. Even in breeds where color is not defined and supposedly carries no influence on how highly the dog is judged, it can matter. A dog show is a show, and in show business flash and glitz count—up to a point, and unofficially; glitz is not mentioned in the standards. A flashy dog—all other things being equal, the dog being well put together with good movement—attracts and holds the attention of the judge and the ringside observers. Surely no judge worthy of the title will overlook cardinal sins like narrow chest, snippy muzzle (pointed when it should be squarish), an overshot or undershot bite, or a dog that paddles or weaves when it moves, just because it has a flashy symmetrical pattern of sharp, bright colors. Glitz also does nothing to excuse bad manners, and a judge with blood dripping from a punctured hand will not likely be intolerant of *pretty* for its own sake.

When the standard for the Beagle says "any true hound color" and for the Borzoi states, "Any color, or combination of colors, is acceptable," a limitation has surely been put on the efficacy of flash. It is nice when it is there, but there are many other things that are far more important. Novices too frequently avail themselves of pet-quality purebred dogs just because they happen to be flashy, and they go into the ring with a dog that is actually loaded with faults that no judge or good, responsible breeder wants to see passed along to the next generation. Bottom line? Flash is pretty, flash is fun, it's great on a leash in your neighborhood, and you can get to meet all kinds of nice new neighbors—fantastic social glue—but glitz's value in the ring is problematical. And, unlike movement and the way the dog is structured from the skeleton out, it tells you nothing of importance about the dog. Remember, in the show ring we are looking for genes that will make this individual dog's puppies as close to 100 percent of the standard as possible.

Flash and glitz should not be confused with condition. They are two very different things. The standards specify what the coat should be like, and it is a matter to which a great deal of attention must be paid. Don't even bother showing a dog whose coat is "blown," not up to standards. A dog is supposed to look terrific, and its coat is a big part of that. An Afghan Hound whose coat isn't elegant and flowing or a Labrador Retreiver who isn't glistening with robust good health might as well hang it up until grooming and diet have brought them up to a competitive level. I have seen many otherwise terrific dogs dumped by the judge because they looked like grubby unmade beds. If ever there was an uninspiring sight, it is an unmade bed going around the ring in company and competition with elegant, glistening hunks.

This is where tone comes into play. No judge prefers

soft, mushy dogs over well-conditioned, well-toned specimens. No matter what its assignment, to be a perpetual motion machine like the Border Collie or a lap sweetie like the
Cavalier King Charles Spaniel, a dog should have exercised
appropriately and be strong and well toned when the cur-
tain goes up.

FAULTS

Those dreadful things called faults can be rather more
precise to deal with than the concept of perfection. There is
usually less opinion involved. It is easier to determine if a
dog has two tails (I am sure that would be considered an un-
forgivable fault) than it would be to determine if a dog's one
and properly only tail is perfect in every respect. Faults are
found in every breed: in the Bichon Frise, cowhocks (where
the midleg joints, or hocks, on the rear legs, turn inward and
the feet turn outward), a snippy muzzle, poor pigmentation,
protruding or yellow eyes, undershot or overshot bite, are all
listed as serious faults for the breed, as are a cockscrew tail
(perish the thought!) and black hair in the coat.

When faults are considered really egregious, they can be
the basis for out-and-out disqualification. The judge is expected to dismiss any Papillon that is more than twelve
inches at the withers (the upper portion of the third to the
sixth dorsal vertebrae, generally called the "shoulder,"
where dogs are "sticked," or measured for height) or if it is
liver colored or if its coat is any solid color, including white.
White patches on the ears or around the eyes and a pink,

spotted, or liver-colored nose will also assure what otherwise might be a handsome little dog an invitation to leave the ring immediately and become a full-time pet. An Italian Greyhound will usually get the old heave-ho if he has tan markings normally found on black-and-tan dogs of other breeds. The lovely little West Highland White Terrier, or Westy, can get into trouble back aft. It is a fault if the tail is set too low on his rump, or if it is too long or carried at half-mast or over the dog's back. The tail is never docked, so a certain length is natural and required. The Westy can also get in trouble up front, since excess timidity and excess pugnacity are both to be discouraged by judges to whom the dog is presented. The German Shepherd Dog is disqualified if it is white in color; if its nose is not predominantly black; if it has cropped or hanging ears, a docked tail, an undershot jaw; or for attempting to bite the judge. (There is now a White German Shepherd Club, but it will be a long time before the AKC or the fanciers of this breed accept the color. The gene that carries white in the German Shepherd is said to carry serious faults as well. But by no means does everyone agree.) In some breeds biting is specified as a kind of ultimate no-no. In no breed is it considered good manners. AKC rules are very specific. Menacing, suggesting that the dog should not be approached and cannot be handled safely, calls for dismissal.

I once watched the judging of a Working Dog breed. There were seven dogs in the ring, and each was goofier than the next. Every time the judge tried to approach a dog, it went ballistic, acting more like a kite on a string than a dog on a lead. The judge walked up and down the line, studying the dogs from a distance and stroking his chin. At the end he dismissed the entire class with the comment that there wasn't a single dog worth pinning a ribbon on at any level. There was a lot of grumbling, but the judge was right.

Among the 160 or so breeds and varieties of dogs recognized for show purposes by the American Kennel Club, there are thousands of details like those above that forever separate show dogs from pet-quality purebred dogs. However, understanding that concept does not assure you of acquiring a show-quality dog. You select your adorable puppy, but some other force will determine what the grown dog will come to be like. Ultimately, you live with and love the dog that fate has designed for your health and hearth. If you can't love your dog, faults and all, you are missing out on a major part of the fun.

Expectations can be high (they usually are in the dog-show world; hope really does spring eternal), expenses can have a brutalizing impact on a family's living standards, travel is intense and costly, but if a judge sees three-quarters of an inch too little ear in an Afghan or a missing black eye rim or any other such catastrophic shortfall, it is back to loving and companionship for the wanna-be show dog and its owner. He or she, or, in short order, *it*, will be kept forever from having a Ch., for Champion, before his name. It's amazing how little the dog itself cares about this.

Random-Bred Dogs

All dogs were once mixed breeds or random-bred, albeit the Bloodhound, Greyhound, Samoyed, Afghan, and many of the others go back centuries or even millennia in pretty much their present forms. A good many breeds that we still recognize attended the birth of the Christian era. Others are quite new. Just about a century ago, for example, Louis Dobermann began breeding what he was sure would be the ultimate police dog in Dortmund, Germany. In fact, his namesake did become a kind of ultimate guard and protection dog. He started his Pinscher with the Rottweiler (a magnificent descendant of the Tibetan Mastiff via Rome), a European Pointer of some kind, and some Terrier, and he added some Greyhound—eventually coming up with the Doberman Pinscher. That is a very different kind of scenario from the Ibizan Hound's, the "Watchdog of the Dead," whose look-alike ancestors with the sacred name Anubis guarded the tombs of pharaohs. The funerary sculptures of Anubis match today's Ibizan Hound standards to an amazing degree.

When is a Doberman Pinscher or any other dog a member of a recognizable breed? When it breeds true, or in other words, when you can have reasonable expectations about what will appear on whelping (birthing) day and in the weeks that follow as the puppy begins to mature. When a dog is "your guess is as good as mine," you have a random-bred dog variously known, disrespectfully and idiotically, I think, as a Heinz 57 (no one shows a pickle—or who knows, maybe they do but in a different context), mutt, cur, pariah, or mongrel, usually muttered with at least a sense of derision. The most derisive comment of all is surely, "Oh, it's just a dog."

What do random-bred dogs have to do with dog shows? Absolutely nothing, and this is not institutionalized hubris or snobbery, either. Leotards and tutus have nothing to do with either ice or field hockey and a palette and easel have nothing to do with ballet. All activities—call them arts, crafts, enthusiasms, sciences, contests, games, sports, fancies, therapies, hobbies, or businesses, as you will—have a core purpose, established rules, and, one hopes, qualified participants. A dog show is all about the best purebred dogs around, and I say that without casting aspersions or looking down a hairy, regal nose.

Ostensibly a dog show's purpose is to single out individual examples of any given breed that are the closest to their own brand of perfection and select them to be mated and produce more and better puppies in kind. This kind of selective breeding has gone on for a very long time, a lot longer than there have been dog shows to memorialize this ultimate contest in opinion.

It is perfectly all right for a show-dog owner to say rude things about a competitor's little pride and joy—they often do—it is accepted, although admittedly rude. In fact, if ruder things are said than those whispered remarks about the competition at a dog show, they will be about the judge.

That is OK. Judges are fair game. However, no one has the right to say anything rude about a random-bred dog. They already have enough on their plate, God love 'em. They need all the respect they can get, for in that way fewer of them might be euthanized.

Showing Your Dog

At the early stages in a dog show the judging is limited to one breed at a time and the field is divided between the sexes. At one point, then, you will have all not-yet-champion, or unfinished, male Cocker Spaniels of a given class in one ring together, all unfinished female English Springer Spaniels in another ring nearby or about to follow the Cockers, and so on through the breeds. Newcomers to the dog-show world don't seem to have difficulty comprehending this system, but later, when the seven groups and Best in Show (BIS) slate are judged, the eyebrows go up. When it seems that a Chihuahua is being judged against a Newfoundland, and a Miniature Poodle against a Bullmastiff, a puzzled expression is the least one could expect. Of course, such judging is never done. No such thing is happening. It just seems that way to the uninitiated. Eventually you end up with seven dogs of seven different breeds (unless it is a one-breed or specialty show). When it gets down to the final contest and the seven group winners are competing for Best in Show, each of the seven dogs is being measured against the standards for its own breed, perfection being worth one hundred points. The judging is not dog against dog but individual dogs against their own breed's standard. (Don't worry if you're not following all this: classes, groups, and judging will be discussed in greater detail in Chapter 3.)

In the Sporting Group ring, then, after the initial judging of the individual breeds, there will be twenty-four breeds represented by one dog or bitch each, in most cases. Each of those dogs will have already won Best of Breed or Best of Variety of its breed earlier that day.

POLITICS IN THE RING

Hang on, now it gets bumpy. The breed we call Cocker Spaniel (a totally different breed today from its ancestor, the English Cocker Spaniel) will be represented not by one dog but by three, each a Best of Variety. One will be black, another will be parti-color (a pinto, of sorts), and the third will be an ASCOB (any solid color other than black). Aside from color, the three Cocker Spaniels will be judged by exactly the same standards. Remember, they are but varieties within a breed.

But hold on, one might say, there is only one Labrador Retriever in the same Sporting Group ring, yet Labs, too, come in three color varieties: black, yellow, and chocolate. Why is there not one of each of them in the ring? The answer is politics. One winner, remember, is chosen for each of the seven groups (winning that coveted ribbon, called Group 1). The hanky-panky that puts three Cocker Spaniels in a Sporting Group ring means that breed has three cracks at Group 1 and hence at the Best in Show judging that follows after all seven Group 1s have been chosen. But the Labrador Retriever will be either black, yellow, or chocolate, and that means that outstanding breed of enormous popularity will have only one shot at Group 1. Depending on the quality of the competition, that can be a definite advantage for the Cocker Spaniel. Nobody said that life is fair.

The same kind of political monkey business appears in the Terrier Group. The wonderfully robust Bull Terrier has both colored and white varieties, and the standards clearly state, "The standard for the colored variety is the same as for the white except for color." I have watched a colored and a white Bull Terrier in the Terrier Group ring that were littermates. The shenanigans involved give that breed an edge, just as with the Cocker Spaniels.

How do these things happen? Most breeds are represented by AKC member clubs and possibly other group and regional clubs as well. Each club sends a delegate to the AKC delegate meetings every year. If a club ("fancy") wants to propose a change in the rules or standards, such changes have to be voted on by all the delegates (460 of them). The Cocker Spaniel and the Bull Terrier people apparently once upon a time had some favors they called in. The changes that do pass are incorporated into the standards, which are then published by the AKC. The politicking that goes on at a delegate meeting is nothing short of awesome.

Some years ago, as the elected delegate of the American Bloodhound Club, I was at the center of an AKC brouhaha.

A delegate representing a hunting dog stood up to oppose my being seated, saying that I would sabotage the hunting sport if I were allowed to sit in their midst. He had done some back-of-the-bench campaigning ahead of time, and some other delegates were convinced that for the sporting fraternity I was the devil incarnate. It was very embarrassing for most of the delegates, the AKC officers, and me. The vote was pushed aside and slated for the next meeting. Finally I was voted in and the delegate who so hated me resigned. (To the best of my knowledge we have never met, which is just fine with me—I don't even remember his name; I presume he had one.) He didn't have to resign, of course, but a lot of people were pleased to see him go. Yes, there are politics in the world of purebred dogs. Big deal! There are politics in Congress, in the Supreme Court, and at the Academy Awards, too.

When It's

Up to the Dog

Chapter

2

One of the most difficult points for a would-be dog person to grasp is the fact (and, yes, it is a fact) that dogs have to really want to show and love to win if they are ever going to do very much of either. In a very real sense, showing off is the dog's call. The next time you watch a dog show, take note of how the winners behave, how they stand (when they are "stacked" by their handlers or self-stacked), and especially how they move. Most standards specify each breed's ideal movement. Here are a few examples:

Pointer: smooth, frictionless, with a powerful hindquarter's drive

Golden Retriever: gait is free, smooth, powerful, and well coordinated

Irish Setter: at the trot the gait is big, very lively, graceful, and efficient

Basset Hound: moves in a smooth, powerful, and effortless manner

Bloodhound: elastic, swinging, and free

Borzoi: front legs must reach well out in front, with pasterns strong and springy

The published standard for each of the breeds goes into far more detail, but these are summary descriptions of what judges look for with their penetrating stare. The point is that the dog's skeleton is 50 percent of the margin between victory and obscurity. If the dog has a weak, malformed, under- or oversize skeleton, it just won't cut it according to the standards. You can hide a lot when a dog is standing still in a show pose ordered up by an expert handler, but you can hide very little once the dog begins to move. Movement in the show ring is one of the most important factors. That's what that moving to and fro is all about. The dog is being judged as a combination of movement and conformation. The coat, often the color, the ears and tail, those are all things to be judged on the outside of the dog. Movement tells you about the inside, the structure of the dog, and each is at least as important as the other. The judge knows exactly what he is looking for. There is a certain amount of hands-on activity that keeps the handler from hiding faults by clever stance or an overdone coat. Ultimately the judge's eyes and hands will pick up on substandard structure and gait, and that dog will be in trouble. I have seen lots of dogs take ribbons I didn't think they deserved for appearance, but I have never seen a klutz get off square one. Show dogs don't trip over their own feet. Handlers do, sometimes, and it is terribly embarrassing. The dogs seem confused when this happens, confused but somehow amused. People at ringside try their best not to giggle.

Then there is the other 50 percent of winning, and that is the dog's attitude and desire to win, that is, to attract attention and be praised. The dog has to have fun, he must be enthusiastic, be excited, respond to applause, and be interested in what is going on or his career will be short and without distinction. The story of our wonderful, sweet Lizzie comes readily to mind. She was the ultimate princess and—oh, my! Didn't she know it!

My wife, Jill, had been having great fun showing Bloodhounds. Ch. The Rectory's Yankee Patriot was our son's great companion and show dog, and my wife was squiring the magnificent slobber-chops around to shows while Clay was in school. There is a lot of standing around and waiting at dog shows, and Jill thought it would be nice to have a second breed to show. Not surprisingly, we decided to find a really fine Basset—show-quality, of course. They are wonderfully amusing dogs; sweet, too. The Bassets would typically be in the ring the same days as the Bloodhounds, in a different ring or, more often, at a different time.

Once launched, our search for a Basset was bound to lead us to Carl Redman, one of the best Basset people in the country. He had a sixteen-month-old bitch he felt was one of the best examples of the breed he had seen in a long time. That was recommendation enough. Carl had recently become a licensed judge and wouldn't be showing anymore, so the incomparable Lizzie could be ours. When we met her I couldn't believe our luck. Lizzie had the Basset's characteristically large head, but she was in that perfect proportion required by her breed's standards. Her coat was hard and smooth and she was a beautiful tricolor—black and white and Hound brown—although in judging Bassets the distribution of color and markings is not taken into account. Her ears were like soft brown velveteen scatter rugs. It seemed that Lizzie offered everything the standard called for: the deep chest, the domed skull, the gaily waving tail, all of it. She was a classically beautiful animal and we couldn't wait until she set the dog world on fire. We were certain that was exactly what she was bound to do. Wait until they saw her out there! We showed her to a couple of the best handlers around and they both said essentially the same thing: "Wow! A Best in Show Basset. I have never seen one like her. This is as good as it gets." Lizzie, although a bit self-centered, was charming with strangers and so pleasant it is hard now to look back and find accurate words to describe her.

Regrettably, it was impossible for Jill and me to make it to her first show because of a prior engagement. So off Lizzie went to the show with her handler and his assistants and several other dogs they would be handling that day. It was like taking the Miss America Pageant on the road. Apparently, although not overly enthusiastic, Lizzie was a lady, until they reached the show grounds, at least. She curled up in her crate and slept all the way there. But then they arrived!

"What in hell is this?" Lizzie seemed to say as strange dogs held on tight leads by strange people with numbers on their arms moved past in a veritable parade. It was a Basset specialty, with a huge number of her kind being shown. To gain any kind of recognition at a specialty show is considered an important happening in a dog's career. Eventually, when she managed to get her nerves under control, Lizzie half walked and was half dragged to the ring, where it was expected she would strut her stuff. Strutting was not exactly what the beauty queen had in mind. She was resentful, disinterested, apparently homesick, and determined to make her handler, whom she barely knew, work for everything he got. She didn't show as much as she sought revenge.

In the ring she went around like a salamander. She hated it, she apparently resented the other dogs and I suspect she gave at least a passing thought to eating the judge's arms when he examined her. I don't think she liked what he did with his hands. The handler said it was the most embarrassing thing that had ever happened to him at a dog show. He said that if he had been judging, he would have given her BIS—not Best in Show but Best in Snake. In fact, to his amazement and ours, the judge did give her a red ribbon, second place in her class. It was an astounding thing, considering her demeanor.

More amazing yet, a few days later we received a letter

from the judge thanking us for the honor of judging a bitch of Lizzie's quality. He said he had seldom seen a dog like her, but he did point out what fun we would have when Lizzie got to like the idea she was presently very busy hating. It was a gracious letter and I have never seen its like in the context of a dog show. We were dubious about this rosy future of which we were being assured, but we were willing to give it our best shot if Lizzie would, too. She wouldn't. No way. Not by half!

We couldn't make it to Lizzie's second show either. Off the troops went again, but when they got to the show grounds, Lizzie took one look around, obviously knew what to expect this time, and seemed to say to her handler: "You just don't get it, do you? The answer is NO! This whole thing is a stupid idea and I think it is yours. Wait until Jill and Roger hear what you are up to. Take me home now, big shot, or I'll show you what one show dog can do to your professional reputation in one afternoon."

This time there was to be no walking and dragging. The poor handler had to carry her to the ring. On the off chance you haven't tried that yourself, carrying an adult Basset across a manicured lawn is like carrying a queen-size, half-filled water bed and then getting it to stay on a towel rack. There is simply no center of gravity. Lizzie grunted and complained all the way down to the ring. She acted more like a camel than a dog, from the reports we got. She did everything but spit. She slobbered instead. The unkind gibing from other handlers and exhibitors did little to raise the handler's spirits or his confidence. Lizzie couldn't have cared less. She was going to have it her way. It was that simple.

There was no letter from a gracious judge this time. Once she got into the ring, Lizzie promptly threw herself onto her back with all four legs in the air and wiggled her hindside in the grass. A good back scratch was just the thing for a disgruntled Basset. While ringsiders gleefully whispered and gossiped, Lizzie was dismissed—charged, I guess, with conduct unbecoming . . .

Lizzie's show career was over, in two shows. She was so unhappy with the scene and so intent on letting us know it that it really would have been cruel to force the issue. A showdown would not have served anyone's purpose. But there was an alternative. Although she would have no show record to boast of or even admit to, she was still a great beauty with impeccable bloodlines. She could produce a litter or perhaps even two litters of beautiful, beautiful puppies from the finest male champion we could find. Puppies such as she would produce would never contribute to the terrible surplus puppy statistics and the ghastly euthanasia rate in this country. That is very important to us and it is something every dog person must always keep in mind. It is of paramount importance. In the case of a fine purebred dog, there is very good reason to breed, as it is well known that people are waiting in line for a puppy. To blame the dog fanciers for the terrible surplus is unfair and wrong. Look to impulse buyers gazing longingly in a pet-shop window and to the pet shop's suppliers, the puppy-mill trade.

The time came and we introduced Lizzie to a splendid male Basset who had been doing very nicely in the ring. He really was an admirable fellow. They were, or at least could have been, a perfect match. He sniffed her and made it clear that he was for the game. He obviously liked her. In fact he was smitten. *She* made it clear that one more jab with an exploring cold nose and she fully intended to eat his face on the spot. To put it mildly, she was distinctly disinterested.

"You want me to do what with whom?"

A short time later we had Lizzie spayed. If the issue had been forced and artificial insemination had been done, Lizzie would probably have been just about as good a mother as she was a show dog. As it was she lived a long, full, loving life on her terms. No one could have wished for a sweeter companion dog than Lizzie. After she was gathered, went on ahead, her slot was taken by another Basset, Pearl, who was so malformed with genetic defects that the veterinarian wanted to put her down. She is making out just fine even though her front legs are more like walrus flippers than dog parts and her tail has a strange sharp-angled bend in it. We have eleven dogs at the moment, eight of which are rescues. Pearl is one of the eight and will never have to worry about showing or whelping. One surgical procedure took care of both concerns. (Spayed and neutered dogs are not shown in conformation competition. Since you are seeking super specimens to further their breeds with superior puppies, there would hardly be any point.)

Lizzie, in retrospect, was a perfect example of that truth

we spoke of. Dogs have to not only like to show but crave it. They have to really want to show off and earn praise. You can't force a dog to perform out there in the ring, nor will it play to the crowd or the judge unless the whole scene pleases it. And it isn't just the bait the handler uses—most often bits of liver baked in the oven on a cookie sheet until hard. (Liver is both the beluga caviar and the Godiva truffles of the hydrant set.) No, it is the liver and the encouraging words and the thumping pats and the people shouting and the chance to interact with the handler, someone the show dog is certain to come to admire. It is a team effort between a dog and its owner or handler. It is a happy time, and a very positive experience has been shared.

People with little experience sometimes think of the dog show as a cruel spectator sport, something like rodeos or diving mules or the Roman arena. Not so, not so at all. Just the opposite is true. Typically, these are dogs that are dearly beloved as pampered family members; for many owners, perhaps most, the showing part is on the second level of importance. First there is the dog and then all the things that follow, including showing, but the displaying and even the pride will always be second on the list for most people. It is the special bond both seek.

Before moving on to other people's dogs, and as a counterpoint to Lizzie, a few words about Yankee are in order. As indicated earlier, Ch. The Rectory's Yankee Patriot was not just a Bloodhound, he was a truly magnificent Bloodhound. I am certain that had his genes been those of a human being, he would have led nations. He weighed about 120 pounds, he was massive and handsome and had incredible place-mat-size ears . . . well, nearly. His disposition left absolutely nothing to be desired. He was wise and gentle and loving. Is it a little goofy to say a dog is *wise*? Maybe. But although that isn't what this book is about, Yankee was wise and showed it in many ways.

On one occasion I recall, a beautiful female Bloodhound named Penny (in fact she was Yankee's daughter) growled a halfhearted warning when my wife nudged her food dish away from the front of the refrigerator. Yankee was standing in the kitchen doorway. He came through the arch like a bolt out of a crossbow and slammed into Penny's side, smashing her against the refrigerator, actually knocking her out. When Penny came to she moved out of the kitchen gingerly, never to growl at anybody again. Yankee went over to the corner and plopped down for a nap. He hadn't made a sound, but he wasn't going to have dogs growling at his people, not on his watch. Not even his own daughter! (A concept, by the way, that he couldn't grasp. Dogs don't comprehend such relationships. They don't need to.)

At nine months, at a show in Maine, Yankee moved up out of the Puppy Class to win the Best of Breed ribbon, and he never looked back. In short order he had his championship, he was on the cover of the *New York Times Magazine*, and his biography was being readied for publication by Putnam. He had it all, a truly splendid animal with brains and personality and incredible good looks. He was substance.

Yankee in the show ring was a wonder to behold. He absolutely loved it and let the world know it. When he was moved around the ring for the judge's approval and the ringside attendees applauded, he would throw his massive head back and yodel a marvelous hound song. Coyotes and wolves are no more musically gifted than Bloodhounds and the Coonhounds that descend from them. The more he *woe-woe-woed*, the more the people would applaud and laugh, and the louder he got. He had so much fun on these occasions I swore he was about to flap his ears and fly right out of the ring and circle overhead. Somehow, I'm not sure how, he knew when he had won yet another ribbon. He *woe-woe-woed* then, too. Bloodhounds are not long-lived, none of the giants are, and when he died at about the age of eight he left a trunkful of ribbons and trophies and a lot of broken hearts in the Caras family and his fan club. There is no doubt in my mind that because Yankee loved to show he did it extremely well, and had he had Lizzie's attitude it wouldn't have mattered what he looked like or how he could have moved. But Yankee had a champion's heart and the stunning good looks to back it up.

Rhonda and Snickers

Rhonda, John, and their two sons live in suburban Baltimore. John did not have dogs growing up; Rhonda did. We know this remarkable story well because in a sense it started right here at our home, Thistle Hill Farm. One warm summer afternoon, poolside with appropriate refreshments, Rhonda had a revelation.

Rhonda and John are close friends of our daughter and son-in-law, Pamela and Joe, and very often the families gather on the farm by the pool. Some of our eleven dogs are always in evidence when the splashing starts and the food arrives. Pamela and Joe usually bring their four dogs, and guests often arrive with theirs. There can be fifteen or more dogs enjoying us as we enjoy them. All of those eating machines in one place at the same time! We like to think of it as a typical American home.

Rhonda regularly interacted with our dogs, and more and more she realized how badly she wanted a dog in her life again. It had been too many years. Coming here reminded her of that fact again and again. That afternoon she and John decided to make the move. Their boys concurred—no great surprise there.

Rhonda had fallen in love with my beautiful golden Whippet named Topaz, Topi to his friends. He is one of my all-time favorite dogs, and where I am, there he is, too. He is a veritable limpet. He and Rhonda spent a lot of time together and Rhonda was determined to own a Whippet of her own. It would be an important part of her family. She and John began surveying dog people in Maryland and Pennsylvania and surrounding states and found a highly regarded breeder in South Carolina who would soon have quality puppies for sale. Rhonda had been ready to accept a mature dog, a rescue, but things went better than planned. They got on the breeder's list (not necessarily an easy thing to do), and with all four family members hopping up and down in anticipation, they waited for their puppy. At eight weeks, generally suggested as the ideal age for a pet dog to go into a new home, Snickers became theirs. There was no plan to show Snickers. She was to be all about love. She had tremendous people skills, and that was more than enough.

When the beautiful, long-dreamed-of Whippet was a few months old, they entered her in a handling class to give their almost-teenage son, Ryan, a new and constructive way to interact with their pet. That is usually a very positive thing to do. Ryan loved Snickers but he hated the discipline of the handling class. Although they had paid for a course of eight classes, Ryan opted out after only two. Rhonda decided that since the other six lessons were already paid for she might as well use them. And what happened next is history.

Friends began pressing Rhonda to show Snickers. It would be a terrible waste, they insisted, not to give Snickers a chance at glory, beautiful girl that she was. Little did they know what lay ahead.

Before she was nine months old, Snickers was in the ring, with Rhonda at the other end of the lead. At the Eastern Whippet Specialty, an important showcase for the breed, Snickers beat thirteen of the fourteen other contenders in a class called Puppy Sweeps under a breeder-judge. Snickers loved showing off, she loved the excitement and the praise. Her gait was, as specified in the standards, free moving and smooth. She looked like a million-dollar Whippet. Elegant is the only word for it, elegant and willing. Snickers came in second, bringing home a bright red ribbon, her first. There were to be many. Rhonda was amazed at what happened, and as she puts it, "I was thrilled that someone else thought my dog was beautiful."

After that initial triumph, Rhonda took Snickers to a couple of other shows just to "see what would happen." Both of the partners in this new enterprise were still highly enthusiastic and still learning. It was a journey of discovery into a new world with new challenges. Rhonda liked the other exhibitors and especially their dogs. She even liked the judges. Secretly, she set to judging all the dogs herself. At ringside she was matching her own eyes against those of the judges. Most observers and contenders at dog shows do that. Dog-show judges are among the most judged people there are.

In Howard County, Maryland, at the fairgrounds, Snickers came under the scrutiny of one of the most awesome judges in America today, or any other day, Anne Rogers Clark. Annie gave Snickers a three-point major—and the lovely, athletic Whippet's course was set. Having Annie Clark lay her broad sword against your shoulder is a kind of ultimate approbation, assuming someone doesn't yell, "Off with his head!" No one knows more about dogs than Annie Clark. Rhonda was still more amazed than anything else.

Ribbon Colors

Specified by the AKC

1st Prize	Blue
2nd Prize	Red
3rd Prize	Yellow
4th Prize	White
Winners	Purple
Reserve Winners	Purple and white
Best of Winners	Blue and white
Special Prize	Dark green
Best of Breed and Best of Variety of Breed	Purple and gold
Best of Opposite Sex to Best of Breed or Best of Variety Best in Show	Red and white

Snickers, after all, was her pet, a very beloved pet by now, a role she happily played for John and the boys, on their own shared turf. Showing was still an extra treat, because the stunningly beautiful sighthound turned out to be so very good at it. Snickers loved it from that first time in Puppy Sweeps at the Eastern Whippet Specialty. She has been for

Defining a Champion

According to the rules of the AKC, a conformation champion is a dog that has won fifteen points, including points from two majors, and those majors must be under two different judges. A major is determined by the number of dogs of that breed and sex that are entered into competition on any given day. One show could be a major for bitches but not for dogs of a breed, or the opposite could be true.

Geography has an awful lot to do with it. A major for Poodles, let us say, will be one thing in Beverly Hills and quite another in Arkansas. In Beverly Hills you are going to have to battle a much larger field of contenders in that breed. And in Arkansas the great Black-and-Tan Coonhound will require more dogs to constitute a major because of the relative popularity of the breed in that part of the country.

It can be difficult to get the necessary majors, and exhibitors help each other out by "making a major," showing extra dogs that are not likely to win, increasing the number of participants of whichever gender is needed. On the other hand, pulling dogs at the last minute can break a major and is generally considered bad manners.

the game ever since. She is, in that sense, a little different from our well-beloved Lizzie. She is exactly the kind of dog that dog shows try to isolate and identify for future breeding. No puppy of Snickers's will be found in pounds and shelters or be scheduled for euthanasia.

So when Anne Clarke gave Snickers her win at the Upper Marlboro Kennel Club in Howard County, Maryland, she gave her one half of her major requirement for life and the first three of the fifteen points she would have to earn before there could be a Ch. before her name in the context of conformation. It was a giant win. Rhonda was both bewildered and ecstatic. She and Snickers were both learning with every step they took. And each was more willing than the other.

Although she is not quite clear why she did it, when Snickers had three of her fifteen points, Rhonda withdrew her from conformation competition. The team went instead for a Field Championship from both the ASFA (American Sighthound Field Association) and the AKC. Snickers went on to earn both titles handily. There was no end to her enthusiasm and thus no stopping her.

It was a rainy afternoon in Bucks County, Pennsylvania, when Snickers reentered conformation competition. She went Winners Bitch, beating thirty-two other Whippet bitches, and earned three more points and now had her two majors under two different judges. She was showing as if a guardian angel were guiding her every pawstep and she was loving it more all the time. Rhonda was jumping-up-and-down happy. Snickers promptly took two more points in Philadelphia. In Bucks County again, a short time later, she went Best of Breed, beating all the Specials, or champions of record, bringing her point count to ten out of the required fifteen. Her next show in Boston took care of that. The beautiful little Whippet who wouldn't stop showing and couldn't stop winning became a champion with two more majors than she needed. Majors can be elusive, as we noted, and it takes some dogs years to get the needed two.

Snickers is now five years old and has had her first litter, five puppies. The sire was Dual Champion Warburton Duke Whittington, FCH, LCM, CD, CAV. It was an entirely suitable match. The puppies were all large at birth, averaging eleven ounces. People across the country have applied to get on the waiting list for a puppy of the brindle-and-white wonder dog. That is virtually always the case when a winner is big-time. Snickers is a known quantity, and a lot of people want to know if her love of the contest carries over to her offspring. Rhonda and John will wait and see. Snickers, the pet, is good at everything she does. Her titles to date:

FCh ASFA: Field Champion, American Sighthound Field Association

FC AKC: Field Champion, American Kennel Club

Multi-BIF: Completed each field title with a Best in Field (equal to a Best in Show)

CH AKC: Conformation Champion, American Kennel Club

CGC AKC: Canine Good Citizen, American Kennel Club

DC AKC: Dual Champion (conformation and field), American Kennel Club

TT: ATTS (American Temperament Test Society)

CD AKC: Companion Dog (obedience title), American Kennel Club

CAV: Champion Award of Versatility, American Whippet Club (AWC); Won: the three AKC champion titles, Conformation, Field, and Obedience

CR WRA: Companion Racer, Whippet Racing Association

TRP, DPC, CWA: Title Racing Proficiency and Dual Purpose Champion, Continental Whippet Alliance

AWC: American Whippet Club winner, National Triathalon Winner

In 1998 Snickers was second Whippet finalist in the AKC National Lure Coursing Championship.

Despite her shortcomings, Rhonda and John have decided to keep Snickers.

All of that and Snickers is still a pet who rolls on her back with her legs in the air whenever a member of her family comes home. She loves guests whether she knows them or not. She is, and this is generally true of Whippets, incapable of assuming a position or pose that is not elegant. She is like fine porcelain. It just so happens that this magnificent little dog with everything in the world going for her loves to show off what she's got, and that makes Rhonda a very happy lady.

A postscript to the comparative stories of Snickers the Whippet and Lizzie the Basset: When it became clear just how well Multi-BIF DC Whippletrees Gold Nugget FCh, CR, CAV, etc. was doing (that's Snickers's registered name), Rhonda and John decided to start another Whippet on the road to advanced stardom. Leia (Surrey Hill Good Girls Don't), one of the most beautiful dogs I have ever seen, was brought into the family. She really is magnificent to look at, and like Snickers is very sweet. There the comparison stops. Leia is just like Lizzie: No way, José. She hates showing, and so the game stops there. She, too, is a princess, a regal couch potato, and you can't help thinking when you look at her, "What a waste." But ultimately the dog does decide. Leia has opted for love and not the rest. She is leaving that to Snickers.

By the way, it isn't a waste. First in order of importance is that loving part. If some dogs like Snickers have it both ways, that's fine, but a dog like Leia is at least as worthy a pooch as the best of them.

Class Act

Chapter

3

Conformation Showing

The AKC licenses or sanctions approximately thirty-three hundred conformation shows a year. There are two styles of show to reckon with: benched and unbenched. At a benched show, to which admission is generally charged, all entered dogs that are twelve months old and older must be "on the bench" throughout the advertised hours of the judging. That means that people who are interested in finding a breed that suits their lifestyle and sense of aesthetics (an enormous number of people attend dog shows for this reason every year) have an opportunity to shop the world of dogs and get to know breeders and handlers personally. It can be a long, tiring day, but an awful lot of dogs, like Snickers, love the excitement of meeting new people and new dogs. It is a highly social event shared by dogs and people.

The benching period usually runs from about nine in the morning to seven or eight in the evening. It is an outstanding opportunity for people who are trying to learn what purebred dogs of show quality are all about, to pick up a month's worth of wisdom in one day. In every sense it is a happening. Regulars sometimes have elaborate picnic equipment, even refrigeration units, that are used for just these events. Old friendships are renewed and new ones are formed. Trivia becomes a species of wisdom, and gossip fills every heart with incredible satisfaction. (*Trivia*, from the Latin, is actually two words: *tri via*, or "three roads." In the old caravan days, what did you find where three roads met? A market and probably a well or surface water. Today you find people showing off their beautiful dogs.) It must be noted that the benched show is an endangered species. There are only eight or nine of them left. Most people opt for the unbenched show. You can still walk around and meet people and look at dogs. It is just that benched shows have always made that a little bit easier to do. It is kind of sad in a way. People don't usually dress up for dog shows either. I liked the old traditional ways. This whole thing of making even dog shows more democratic takes its toll in grandeur. At least the dogs are still grand, even if the people are not. That can never change.

Most of the people who avail themselves of this opportunity to see it all with the hope of one day knowing it all are practically walking on the sides of their ankles by the time the whole thing breaks up in the evening. But leaving, they know a great deal more about dogs than they did coming. If they make a good impression, they might even have managed to get their names put on an important breeder's list for a future puppy. That can be step number one in a dream's coming true.

At a dog show you can avail yourself of vendors' booths with leashes and collars, stainless steel bowls, grooming supplies, toe nail clippers, brushes and combs and blow dryers; book stalls with nothing but dog books, of which there are an endless number; art and antiques dealers who specialize in dog art and figurines. Breed-oriented T-shirts abound, and bumper sticker artisans and crate-label, flag, and banner specialists are all there to be of service. There are more ways to make a buck off a dog than most novices realize.

In the larger shows major dog-food companies have elaborate displays telling you why you should use their products. They give out free samples for your dog to evaluate. Free literature that the manufacturers tell you will guide you toward good canine nutrition and their products is available everywhere. There are kiosks with computer games you can play that will call forth breed information and other doggy data. By the end of the day, if you are not selective, you will have instructions on how to do just about anything that is dog oriented, free samples of all kinds, monstrously overpriced cold-cast bronze figurines of your breed, and 1950s ashtrays also depicting your breed. You can also buy bird feeders, although the connection is, I think, vague. It is, you learn, addictive. It is a good idea to bring a folding cloth shopping bag on one of these expeditions. You'll need it. A caddie to carry it and a therapist to massage your feet and ankles at the end of the day are personal options. You can do this thing, this plunge into dogdom, as simply or as elegantly as you want. However elegant you want to be yourself, all the dogs around you will be—elegant, that is.

With all of the coming and going, there is a bit of a carnival atmosphere. (Be careful where you step.) As you will probably note, it is amazing how few dogfights there are. That is always surprising to newcomers. People are extremely careful, however, that their dogs don't get their leashes crossed or tangled with those of other dogs. That kind of mix-up can lead to absolute mayhem. Anyone not completely in charge of his dog is looked down upon by all the other participants. Dogs and people at a dog show are expected to be on their best behavior.

Of course, there are people-food vendors, too. You can smell your way to them as surely as a Bloodhound or a pack of thirteen-inch Beagles can. There is a lot of tradition here. The cheeseburgers are characteristically vile, while the barbecue pork on a bun is not only poisonous but ruinous to your cleaning bill. People with mustard, ketchup, and barbecue sauce on their chins and shirt fronts are everywhere. Still, traditions are essentially nice things to have, and the dog-show world is full of them.

Mordecai Siegal is the respected six-time president of the Dog Writers Association of America (DWAA) and very much involved in matters doggy. He is kind of a Wolf Blitzer of the hydrant set. I asked him to define a dog show as he knew it. "It is many things to me," he said. "It is part competition, part exhibition, and part yard sale. It is part circus, part bazaar, and a good part great entertainment. The show part is a very important, very meaningful social event."

Most shows today are unbenched. Dogs arrive in time for their moment of glory in the ring, and if they don't win early in the proceedings and therefore have no chance to move on up the ladder later that day, they can leave as soon as they are out of the ring. The cheeseburgers are no better than at the benched shows. The dogs, of course, are just as nice; that is a given—splendid companion canines that are variously beautiful enough or handsome enough to make showing them off one of the most compelling forces in the lives of their human partners.

THE CLASSES

Whereas groups divide breeds by type (see "The AKC Recognized Breeds" sidebar in this chapter), the class is the entry level, the first stage in any regular conformation show. It is where all dogs start out on their climb to stardom—and unfortunately, it is where a good many end up. It is where enthusiasm, hope, and dreams have to face off with reality and truth, condition, and more than a bit of luck. (I've watched a lot of people ringside, and it always seems to me they are praying. I don't know if that helps or not, but perhaps it's like chicken soup—it couldn't hurt.)

Dogs, except for established champions, are shown in

one or more of seven regular classes. Most of the shows you will attend will feature all seven classes, but on occasion one or more can be missing, although that is the exception rather than the rule. Dogs cannot be entered in any given class if they are a day under or a day over the designated age. In such matters in the world of dog shows there are no approximations.

In the United States dogs (and bitches, of course) are entered in only one of the first six classes. (In England they may be in more than one class at a time.) First is the Puppy Class, for dogs six months old and older, but under twelve months. This class is sometimes further divided into six to nine months and then nine to twelve months.

Dogs older than twelve but under eighteen months that are not already champions can be entered in the Twelve-to-Eighteen-Month Class.

The Novice Class is for dogs that are at least six months old but don't as yet have any of the fifteen points needed for the championship designation. It is another classification for beginners, a way in and, it is hoped, a way to start the climb that in the end will put a Ch. in front of the dog's name. AKC rules state that a dog can't be entered in this class if it has already won three first-place ribbons in Novice or a first place in American-Bred or Bred-by-Exhibitor.

The entrants in the Bred-by-Exhibitor Class (often shortened to Bred-By) must have been whelped in the United States, or if whelped outside of the United States, they must have been registered in the AKC studbook. They must be at least six months old, they cannot be champions, and they must be owned wholly or in part and handled by the person or spouse of the person who was the breeder or one of the breeders of record. It is a kind of ultimate family affair. (A studbook, of course, is, as its name implies, a record of what bitch had what puppies as a result of a liaison with which proud dog. It is a kind of nonfiction romantic novel. Of course, assigning numbers to these things takes much of the romance out of it.)

The American-Bred Class is for dogs older than six months (excluding champions) that were born (whelped) in the United States from a breeding that also occurred in the United States. (It is all very chauvinistic!)

The popular Open Class is for any dog six months or older. In the case of a specialty show, the club sponsoring the show can designate that for that one show the Open Class is for American-Bred dogs only.

Those are the first six regular classes that more or less begin the climb upward toward Best in Show in all conformation shows. The dogs entered are generally younger dogs, but one or more of them may be the most stunning dogs in the whole show. Still, they must go up through the classes until they are champions of record. The "class dogs" cannot be champions, or finished. That is what they are in those six classes for.

Important point: Which class, since there is clearly very often a choice, does an exhibitor pick for his dog? The class where the dog has the best chance of winning. It would probably be a poor idea to take an immature, puppyish dog and plunk it down in Novice, where it will have to compete with dogs that are more mature and probably more experienced. In American-Bred or Bred-By there may be just a few entries, while in the same show there may be twenty dogs in Novice or Open. I have seen as few as one or two dogs in a class. Unless your dog has his head on backward or his tail in the middle of his chest, he is likely to win if he has no competition—not guaranteed to win, but with a chance.

All right then, the first six classes have been judged, once for dogs and once for bitches for every breed represented in the show, and you have all those eager winners and their handlers. This is when the Winners Class comes into being. It comprises all the dogs that have won a blue ribbon for their breed and gender in any of the six classes. There will potentially be a Winners Dog and a Winners Bitch for each breed and class.

From the Winners Class, the Best of Breed selection will be made. At this point the breakdown by sex is no longer in force. Competitors include all the Winners by breed from all classes, plus any champions of record that now enter into the competition. The overall winner gets the Best of Breed or Best of Variety of Breed ribbon.

After the Best of Breed has been determined, the Best of Opposite Sex title will be awarded. Best of Opposite is simple. If a dog wins Best of Breed or Variety, a bitch is chosen for the Opposite title. And, of course, vice versa. The Best of Opposite is equivalent to saying that the dog would have been Best of Breed if the actual winner had been absent.

Finally, the Best of Winners will be chosen. Each Winners Dog and Winners Bitch for each breed, representing all the first six classes, will be judged and the Best of Winners Chosen. The Best of Winners title holder gets the points set for Winners Dog or Winners Bitch, whichever is greater, calculated by the number of entries.

Everything that has happened up to now has been setting the stage. The points are awarded and all those Winners dogs move closer to their championships. In some cases, some dogs will finish—complete their championship requirements—either with needed points or with a missing major win (remember, two majors are needed under two different judges).

All of this is not as jumbled and confusing as it may seem. It is considerably worse. Nothing daunted, the trick is to stroke one's chin and say *ummmm* as convincingly as possible. Just look wise. Mutter words like *interesting* and *profound, cool* and *daring*. No one will seriously challenge you. The people around you will be just as confused as you are. No problem, admire all the beautiful dogs and have fun—most of them are (the dogs, that is). The only ones who seem to understand all this or not care a fig if they don't are the dogs. The exhibitors just think it is their day in the sun; the dogs know it belongs to them. Everyone gets a chance to be a happy camper. After all, if the owner and the dog aren't both happy, why go through the whole thing? Why spend the money? Buy a boat instead and enter a regatta. You don't have to housebreak a Boston whaler. As for the competition, the AKC registers nearly a million and a quarter new purebred puppies a year. Theoretically, all of them could be entered in shows and compete. All told, there are about eleven thousand licensed and sanctioned AKC events (including conformance and field shows) every year.

THE FINAL JUDGING

Now comes the group judging, and this is pretty clear-cut. The Best of Breed or Variety, dog *or* bitch, for each breed is automatically entered into one of seven group competitions—Sporting Dogs, Nonsporting Dogs, Working Dogs, Herding Dogs, Hounds, Terriers, Toys—and is judged simultaneously with its counterpart winners from every other breed in its group. The Group 1 ribbons go to one presumably spectacular dog in each of the seven groups. There are second-, third-, and fourth-place ribbons in each group, too. Although highly coveted and well and truly boasted, these group placements, other than first, do not carry the winners any further in that particular show. Exciting though it may be to earn a group placement, they are still the dogs that went almost all the way. They have, though, done very well and will be watched in the future by that breed's fanciers.

When the seven groups have been judged, there are seven dogs left. They are then judged for the ultimate accolade, Best in Show, and that is as good as it gets. Those seven finalists may have started out as part of a crew of thousands of dogs on the opening morning, so getting down to one of seven is no small thing. It is awesome. The peak of the pyramid is in sight.

A legitimate question: If an established champion doesn't need any more points than he has already won, and thereby has his title for all time, why is he entered with class dogs for Winners and Best of Breed ribbons? Simple. There is always the chance he can go all the way, take his Group 1, and then go on to win Best in Show. He is, after all, a proven dog with his championship. The title Best in Show is truly coveted, and when a dog can be described as a Best in Show winner, the finest breeding partners and the best handlers get in line. So do checkbooks. It is a matter of building a reputation win by win, and that is one thing no show dog or dog owner can ever have too much of: winning. Those wins are added up, and few things sound sweeter to a dog exhibitor than "top winning sporting dog of the year" or even "top winning American Water Spaniel of the year." It is like Wall Street in a sense; greed is the operative word. But it is a nice, warm, fuzzy greed in which man and dog can rejoice. At its best, *ecstasy* is the operative word.

THE MECHANICS OF SHOWING

The mechanics and sociology of the dog ring are not really all that difficult to master. The psychology can be a bit tricky and trying, but the nuts and bolts are not nearly as tough as a bridge game and are easier than following a Martha Stewart recipe.

You must enter your dog at least two and a half weeks prior to the show date as indicated in the premium—a printed list mailed in advance to entrants. You can variously fax, mail, or even e-mail some superintendent's office to enter your dog for conformation judging. Once you have entered your dog, you will receive a program of the judging schedule by mail. You should have it in your hands about a week before the show. This includes travel directions, your ring number and time, and the number of dogs entered in each breed. You can easily determine whether there are enough dogs or bitches to constitute a major.

The judging breaks down the entry of the dogs in each breed as in the following example:

30 Akita 10–15 (3–2)

That is not from a World War II Nazi encoding machine like Enigma. It very simply states that thirty Akitas are entered for the show that you will be attending. Of those, twenty-five are class dogs (not yet finished), ten males and fifteen females. In addition, there will be five champions competing for Best of Breed, three males and two females.

Dogs are not identified by names, as that could have an impact on your decision about attending. Allow two to three minutes per dog to estimate the time you need to arrive if your breed is not the first in the ring as listed in the schedule. Remember, dogs always precede bitches. If some dogs are pulled, you may be expected in the ring earlier, so be there with time to spare. Personally, I hate cutting it close. Think about traffic, getting lost, getting a flat, and going into the ring with your stomach already in a knot. Be merciful to yourself and your dog. Get there an hour or two early, visit with friends, drink coffee, bring along a bag of bagels and doughnuts and share them.

If your dog is going to require any grooming, get there really ahead of time. You have to check in and get your armband, and it isn't a bad idea to watch the judge you will be facing at work—see what he or she does. (Just as likely, it will be *she*.) It will usually be the same for all dogs showing under him. The more you know about him the better you are likely to do.

The ring steward is responsible for running an efficient ring. He or she manages the ring activities for the judge. The steward begins each breed by calling out each of the seven regular classes, beginning with puppy dogs. The handlers are expected to be ringside for their class judging. Stewards can often be heard ringside calling out "Puppy dog six to nine months, number twenty-one" as a last call prior to the start of judging for absent entries, but only as a courtesy, so be ready when it's your turn to enter the ring. If you are not present when your class is called, you will probably forfeit your entry fee and the chance to show your dog that day, however much traveling you have had to do.

Typically, the judge will ask that dogs line up in catalog order. If you watch your judge evaluate the breed prior to your appearance, you can gain a pretty good sense of his style and ring procedure. Once he judges the first dog in your breed, he will judge every dog using the same moving pattern. As the dogs stand in the initial lineup, the judge will generally walk down the line and look at the overall structure of the entries. Many judges will use this opportunity to look for any obvious visible breed disqualifications, such as coat appearance, eye color, height, and so forth. He may also note appealing features such as expression or attitude.

Once the judge completes the initial assessment of the class entries, he will ask the handlers to move the dogs around the entire ring together once or twice. This is his first opportunity to evaluate your dog's gait and soundness as compared with the standards for the breed. When the circuit is completed, the judge will expect the first dog to be stacked—set up in the show stance—on the ground or on a table, depending on the size of the breed or the judge's personal preference, for a hands-on examination. Judges typically step back and look at the dog's general structure again during this individual exam. He may approach from the side or front, allowing the dog to see him before he touches it. Typically, the judge looks at the head and the eyes before he examines the bite—the way the teeth come together. It is always a pleasure to see a dog lick the judge as if to say, "Pick me, me, not the others, me!"

The judge completes the hands-on evaluation, going over the dog's head, neck, shoulders, front assembly, chest, top line, croup (rump), hindquarters, tail, and coat, comparing every aspect of the dog to the specific breed standards.

Testicles are the last things examined—males only, of course. The judge often steps back for a final look, comparing the dog to his or her interpretation of the standards. The handler must be alert and follow the judge's moves. The dog must look its best at all times from every angle.

The handler is asked to move the dog by itself in a pattern, most often either a triangle, down and back, or both. The judge is looking at the dog's front movement for correctness, as well as watching the dog move away and observing its top line and overall carriage.

The triangle allows the judge to evaluate all aspects of the dog's gait, including the side gait. Each handler has to experiment to determine the best pace to move the dog to show it off to its greatest advantage. You will hear judges remind handlers to slow down or move at a more moderate pace, leaving plenty of room for other exhibitors if the lineup is moving together. There are few things worse than showing a dog and having another handler run up on you. Your dog hates it, too. Very bad manners!

The dog will finish the individual gaiting by free or self-stacking in front of the judge. This is where you see handlers baiting and throwing liver treats to improve their dogs' expressions and show their very best attributes. Watch experienced handlers. They are artists working with animated sculpture. They know how to accentuate the most positive features of their dogs in the free stack. The individual exam ends with the handler moving the dog around the ring in a circle, with an emphasis on showing off the side gait—the gait as viewed from the side. The judge goes into the next dog's individual exam. If your dog is the only entry in the class, and that does happen, the judge directs you to a place marker and hands you the blue ribbon, if you deserve first place. It is a real downer when he doesn't. When you can't win even with no competition, rethink what you are doing. You can also show cats, cows, mules, horses, and rabbits— even canaries, koi, and goldfish.

Once the judge examines every dog in the class, all the dogs line up for a final time in picture-perfect stacked position. Handlers are working here to keep their dogs attentive and maintain a standing position that shows off their overall appearance. Often judges will have all entries or selected dogs move again to crystallize their choices. They may ask the entire class to move again individually or all together before designating their final picks. Remember to leave plenty of room for other exhibitors. This is no time for you to exhibit your bad manners. The judge makes his selections, pointing to exhibitors and calling out class placements. Pay careful attention and look at the judge as placements are called. Many a fidgety handler has missed the judge's final choices while fussing over the dog's final stack.

The judge selects his winner for each of the six dog classes. All six class winners are then called back into the ring by the steward to compete for Winners Dog (WD). Typically, the judge will briefly examine each winner again and often move each winner individually. Finally, the judge points to a Winners Dog. This is the dog that receives the coveted points toward its championship. The number of points is based on the actual number of dogs defeated that day. Excused or absent dogs do not count in the point calculations. Points are awarded differently on a regional basis and change from year to year based on the AKC schedule and the dogs competing the year prior to your show date. You can always ask the steward following judging how many points you received for winning the blue.

The steward calls out the second-place dog (if any) from the class the Winners Dog just left. This dog now competes with the other class winners for Reserve Winner. The Reserve Winner is considered the next-best dog competing that day in the classes but does not get points.

The bitch classes now follow the dog entries until the judge points to the Winners Bitch (WB), which is the only other entry to receive points at the show. Now the steward calls out the Specials (champion dogs and bitches) to compete along with the Winners Dog and Winners Bitch for Best of Breed. Each champion of record is examined in the same manner as the class dogs and bitches. All of this is carried out for each breed individually.

All Best of Winners will compete later in the day (or perhaps the next day if the show is a large, multiday event) with the other Best of Breed winners within their group for one of four placements in the group ring. Here the competition is very stiff, as the Breed winner is often up against top contenders. The entries can come from all over the United States, Puerto Rico, and Canada.

The AKC Recognized Breeds

No one knows how many pure breeds there are still left in the world. A great many breeds have become extinct over the centuries. I have seen the top figure for survivors given as both 450 and 850. No doubt before the final count is made, many of the breeds here today will be gone, exterminated by lack of interest on our part. (When a breed vanishes, a distressing amount of our own history and culture goes with it.) Some others will have come into being during this time, although why we need more is beyond my understanding. There are certainly breeds enough now on this planet for every season, for every task, and for love.

The breeds and varieties now recognized by the AKC are fewer than 170 in number. The AKC breeds with their probable or known lands of origin are listed here in their proper groups.

Group 1: Sporting Dogs—24 Breeds, 3 Varieties

Brittany (formerly known as Brittany Spaniel)	France
Pointer	Europe/Britain
Pointer, German Shorthaired	Germany
Pointer, German Wirehaired	Germany
Retriever, Chesapeake Bay	United States
Retriever, Curly-Coated	?
Retriever, Flat-Coated	Britain/Canada
Retriever, Golden	Britain
Retriever, Labrador	Newfoundland

Setter, English	British Isles
Setter, Gordon	Scotland
Setter, Irish	Ireland
Spaniel, American Water	United States
Spaniel, Clumber	British Isles
Spaniel, Cocker (three varieties)	United States
ASCOB	
Black	
Parti-color	
Spaniel, English Cocker	British Isles
Spaniel, English Springer	British Isles
Spaniel, Field	British Isles
Spaniel, Irish Water	Ireland
Spaniel, Sussex	British Isles
Spaniel, Welsh Springer	Wales
Vizsla	Hungary
Weimaraner	Germany
Wirehaired Pointing Griffon	Holland

Group 2: Hounds—23 Breeds, 5 Varieties

Afghan Hound	Afghanistan
Basenji	Africa
Basset Hound	France/Belgium
Beagle (two varieties)	British Isles
Up to 13 inches	
13 to 15 inches	

Black-and-Tan Coonhound	British Isles/United States
Bloodhound	Mediterranean
Borzoi (formerly Russian Wolfhound)	Russia
Dachschund (three varieties)	Germany
Longhaired	
Smooth	
Wirehaired	
Foxhound, American	British Isles/United States
Foxhound, English	British Isles
Greyhound	Ancient Egypt
Harrier	Europe/British Isles
Ibizan Hound	Egypt
Irish Wolfhound	Ancient Rome/Ireland
Norwegian Elkhound	Norway
Otterhound	British Isles
Petit Basset Griffon Vendeen	France
Pharaoh Hound	Malta
Plott Hound	United States
Rhodesian Ridgeback	Southern Africa
Saluki	Arabia
Scottish Deerhound	Scotland
Whippet	British Isles

Group 3: Working Dogs—20 Breeds

Akita	Japan
Alaskan Malamute	Alaska
Bernese Mountain Dog	Switzerland
Boxer	Germany
Bullmastiff	Britain
Doberman Pinscher	Germany
Giant Schnauzer	Germany
Great Dane	Germany
Great Pyrenees	France/Spain
Greater Swiss Mountain Dog	Switzerland
Komondor	Hungary
Kuvasz	Hungary
Mastiff	Britain
Newfoundland	British Isles
Portuguese Water Dog	Portugal
Rottweiler	Germany
Saint Bernard	Switzerland
Samoyed	Siberia/Arctic
Siberian Husky	Siberia/United States
Standard Schnauzer	Germany

Group 4: Terriers—26 Breeds, 4 Varieties

Airedale Terrier	British Isles
American Staffordshire Terrier	British Isles
Australian Terrier	Australia
Bedlington Terrier	British Isles

Border Terrier	British Isles
Bull Terrier (two varieties)	British Isles
Colored	
White	
Cairn Terrier	British Isles
Dandie Dinmont Terrier	British Isles
Fox Terrier, Smooth	British Isles
Fox Terrier, Wire	British Isles
Irish Terrier	Ireland
Jack Russell Terrier	British Isles
Kerry Blue Terrier	Ireland
Lakeland Terrier	British Isles
Manchester Terrier (two varieties)	British Isles
Standard, 12 to 22 pounds	
Toy (shown in Toy Group)	
Miniature Bull Terrier	British Isles
Miniature Schnauzer	Germany
Norfolk Terrier	British Isles
Norwich Terrier	British Isles
Scottish Terrier	Scotland
Sealyham Terrier	British Isles
Skye Terrier	British Isles
Soft-Coated Wheaten Terrier	Ireland
Staffordshire Bull Terrier	British Isles
Welsh Terrier	Wales
West Highland White Terrier	British Isles

Group 5: Toys—20 Breeds, 9 Varieties

Affenpinscher	Europe
Brussels Griffons (two varieties)	Belgium
Long-Coat	
Smooth-Coat	
Cavalier King Charles Spaniel	British Isles
Chihuahua	Mexico and Asia?
Chinese Crested	China
English Toy Spaniel (two varieties)	British Isles
Blenheim and Prince Charles	
King Charles and Ruby	
Havanese	Cuba (and ?)
Italian Greyhound	Greece/Turkey/Italy
Japanese Chin	Japan
Maltese	Malta
Manchester Terrier (two varieties)	British Isles
Standard (in Terrier Group)	
Toy, not over 12 pounds	
Miniature Pinscher	Germany
Papillon	Spain/Italy
Pekingese	China
Pomeranian	Iceland/Lapland
Poodle (three varieties)	Germany/France?
Miniature	
(in Nonsporting Group)	
Standard	
(in Nonsporting Group)	
Toy, up to 10 inches	

Pug	China/Netherlands
Shih Tzu	China
Silky Terrier	Australia
Yorkshire Terrier	British Isles

Group 6: Nonsporting Dogs—16 Breeds, 3 Varieties

American Eskimo Dog	United States
Bichons Frise	Canaries/Spain
Boston Terrier	United States
Bulldog	British Isles
Chinese Shar-Pei	China
Chow Chow	China
Dalmatian	?
Finnish Spitz	Finland
French Bulldog	France
Keeshond	Netherlands
Lhasa Apso	Tibet
Lowchen	Germany
Poodles (three varieties)	Spain/France/Germany
Miniature, 10 to 15 inches	
Standard, over 15 inches	
Toy (in Toy Group)	
Schipperke	Belgium
Shiba Inu	Japan
Tibetan Spaniel	Tibet
Tibetan Terrier	Tibet

Group 7: Herding Dogs—18 Breeds, 2 Varieties	
Anatolian Shepherd Dog	Turkey
Australian Cattle Dog	Australia
Australian Shepherd	United States
Bearded Collie	Scotland
Belgian Malinois	Belgium
Belgian Sheepdog	Belgium
Belgian Tervuren	Belgium
Border Collie	Scotland
Bouvier des Flandres	France
Briard	France
Canaan Dog	Israel
Collie (two varieties)	British Isles
Rough	
Smooth	
German Shepherd Dog	Germany
Old English Sheepdog	British Isles
Puli	Hungary
Shetland Sheepdog	British Isles
Welsh Corgi, Cardigan	Wales
Welsh Corgi, Pembroke	Wales

Next is judging for Best in Show. This is as good as it gets in the dog-show world, winning the red-white-and-blue BIS ribbon and achieving the top spot of the day, defeating all other show entries. Breeders, owners, and handlers value this award and feel a great sense of accomplishment when their dog is judged to be the finest dog at either an all-breed or a specialty show.

O'er Land and Sea

The interlocking of the dog fancies in the United Kingdom and the United States, something that seems so logical, has remained a lopsided affair at best. The English, Scotch, Irish, and Welsh have created and maintained some of the best breeds and some of the finest individual dogs in the world. They are masters of the craft and extremely enthusiastic. Bloodlines from the British Isles have contributed more to our best dogs than those from any other country. All of the dogs in the Terrier Group, for example, with the exception of the Miniature Schnauzer, were developed in the United Kingdom, then transported here. No fewer than thirteen of the Sporting Dog breeds are listed with the British Isles as their country of origin.

It would make sense for the two countries, the United States and the United Kingdom, to exchange dogs, enter into each other's most important shows, and cross bloodlines—within the breeds, of course. That is not how it works, however. British breeders and fanciers can send their dogs here anytime they want with nothing more than a forty-eight-hour-old veterinary health certificate, but there it stops. Any dog sent to the United Kingdom from here has to go into a usually dreadful six-month quarantine. Not only are our dogs banned there, but an English owner coming here has to face the same monstrous nonsense when he tries to take his pet back home. Few owners care to do that to their friend, so relatively few dogs get to enter the United Kingdom if they have even set paw in the United States.

The fuss is over rabies, and the British are downright paranoid on the subject. The disease has been eradicated in the United Kingdom, but we still have it here, of course. If dogs are up-to-date on their rabies shots, however, an active infection is extremely unlikely. It is difficult to imagine a Toy Poodle or a Maltese or a Pekingese living in a Park Avenue penthouse being exposed at all. Still, the British have not been just firm on this subject, they have been absolutely rigid, and the wonderful interchange that should exist has never been possible. Just what impact this has all had on the world of purebred dogs here and in the United Kingdom is difficult to imagine. It is clearly a negative when viewed from any angle.

Dog fanciers on this side of the Atlantic have been just as adamant over the matter and have been demanding new regulations. The British government has refused to budge an inch. Now, at the beginning of the twenty-first century, dog lovers in many parts of the world are rejoicing. The quarantine rule is about to be modified. Dogs from some countries will be able to enter the United Kingdom without quarantine. Unfortunately, North America's show dogs and pets won't be set free even under the new regulations. The exchange will still be one way when it comes to the United States, Mexico, and Canada. Jill and I have brought two wonderfully bred and cared-for dogs over from England, a Bulldog and a West Highland White Terrier, but when we moved to London for a while in 1965, none of our dogs came with us. Government bureaucracy has once again managed to create an unnecessary glitch in the way people and their dogs live. But then, that is why God invented bureaucrats in the first place. If woman was harvested from man's body—the ribs—I have a suggestion as to what parts were used to assemble the first bureaucrat. Not here, however. We should be alone for that discussion.

The Miscellaneous Class

Over the years, slowly but surely, the breeds recognized by the AKC have grown in number. There is a simple, entry-level procedure that makes this possible. It is called the Miscellaneous Class. It is a thing apart from the seven regular *groups*, but it has the same long-range purpose and plan. The number of breeds usually included at any one time awaiting recognition and a chance for their place in the sun is not specified.

The studbook at the AKC is not sitting around wringing its hands waiting for people to come up with ideas for new breeds to fill the niches and columns in the seven groups. Just the opposite is true. There are no niches, as such. In fact, there is considerable resistance to new breeds, particularly when they are cutesy home-grown things like Cockapoos, Peekypoos or Poopypekes and Peekycocks. There are

The Move from Miscellaneous Class to a Regular Group and Championship Points

1980:	Australian Cattle Dogs*	Working Group
1984:	Pharaoh Hound	Hound Group
	Portuguese Water Dog	Working Group
	Tibetan Spaniel	Nonsporting Group
1988:	Finnish Spitz	Nonsporting Group
1991:	Petit Basset Griffon Vendeen	Hound Group
	Chinese Crested	Toy Group
	Chinese Shar-Pei	Nonsporting Group
1992:	Miniature Bull Terrier	Terrier Group
1993:	Australian Shepherd Dog	Herding Group
	Shiba Inu	Nonsporting Group
1995:	American Eskimo Dog	Nonsporting Group
	Greater Swiss Mountain Dog	Working Group
	Border Collie	Herding Group
1996:	Cavalier King Charles Spaniel	Toy Group
1997:	Canaan Dog	Herding Group
1999:	Havanese	Toy Group
	Lowchen	Nonsporting Group
	Anatolian Shepherd Dog	Herding Group
2000:	Jack Russell Terrier	Terrier Group
	Plott Hound	Hound Group

*In 1983 the breed was moved over to the newly formed Herding Group, where it is today.

81

plenty of cute dogs in the appropriate groups already. As random-bred dogs, such critters can be and frequently are sweet and rewarding pets, but they are not needed and have no possible role to play in the world of purebred dogs, particularly among show-quality purebred dogs. They cannot be shown, needless to say. They are very often toy-size creations affectionately known as patio lice. At Thistle Hill Farm half of our dogs are large, but I refer to our smallish herd of small terriers as army ants. Call them what you will, millions of dogs and puppies every year are killed for the want of suitable homes. It is cruel to purposely create more of them. Cute won't always save a dog's life down at the pound, sad to report.

To get heretofore unrecognized breeds (in the United States) into the Miscellaneous Class, a group of fanciers (enthusiasts) have to follow the drill. First they have to prove that what they have is indeed a breed unto itself, breeding true. (As far as I know, the number of generations for breeding true is nowhere specified.) They must offer proof that there is substantial and widespread interest in the breed and that there is activity surrounding the proposed breed. There has to be an active club that maintains a breed registry, with the breeding activity expanding over a wide area in the United States.

When the AKC board of directors (collectively, those olde wise men of the hydrant set) decides these conditions have been met, the breed can be admitted to the Miscellaneous Class. It can now participate in AKC obedience trials and even earn obedience titles. These breeds are not eligible for championship points, however, although they are shown without points in some conformance shows. Eventually the AKC board will decide there is enough activity and the new breed will be admitted to one of the seven regular groups. Once the breed is in a group, it will follow the trail all show dogs follow, developing its own great champions and legends. It must be understood that the "new" breed may in fact be hundreds or even thousands of years old in other countries or areas. *New*, as used here, means new to us, and we are not always the first to know.

A case in point is the PBGV. This Basset-size, fuzzy scent hound is run in hunting packs and has been for an estimated four hundred years in France, Denmark, and the Netherlands. The initials stand for Petit Basset Griffon Vendeen. It is generally referred to as the happy breed. After nearly four centuries of popularity, it became a recognized breed by the Kennel Club in Great Britain. In short order it was recognized in Canada, and after building in popularity there, it was moved out of the Miscellaneous Class into the Hound Group in the Canadian Kennel Club (CKC). That had nothing to do with the AKC, yet. The PBGV is a hound in a terrier coat, with more than a little terrier in its style and outlook on life. We got our two from Canada because they were then so hard to find here. That is rapidly changing. After its success in Canada the PBGV repeated the process in the United States, where it has now moved from the Miscellaneous to the Hound Group. (Having lived with a couple of PBGVs for years, I am convinced that they are every bit as much Terrier as Hound.)

There are mixed feelings about "new" dogs being accorded AKC recognition. There is frequently a horrendous, vituperative battle between club factions, those who want recognition and those who do not. It is often said that recognition leads to rapidly expanding popularity, and that leads to careless breeding practices by puppy mills who supply the pet shops with ghastly, substandard puppies. There is also an inevitable touch of snobbery: keeping a good thing to ourselves. It is generally felt by a great many fanciers that they "don't need" AKC recognition, that it is beneath them and their dogs. This split in opinion can get nasty at times and may delay a breed's recognition for years. It is often a very hot issue in the politics of the dog-show world. It has brought more than a few old friendships tumbling down. Think of it as the Blue and the Gray all over again, brother against brother, father against son. Dog people have tight collars (their own, not their dogs'), and it can get a bit on the steamy side when opinions differ.

On the subject of recognition, a lot of dog fanciers are attracted to the concept of ground floor. The thought of being one of the first in the land to own a newly recognized breed or even a not-yet-recognized breed is adventuresome. These are the breeders who will eventually determine the breed's standards.

As of this writing (1999–2000: close to the start of a new millennium) five new breeds have come on line in just one year. The massive Anatolian Shepherd Dog at 150 pounds is a true giant of the dog world. The Canaan Dog from Israel is unique in that it existed as a herder in ancient times. Feral examples of the breed lived on in the desert and then, from the 1930s on, specimens were recaptured as "wild" dogs and redomesticated. It is the only redomestication we know of. Someday, we can imagine, that could happen with the dingo in Australia.

A lovable companion dog known as the Lowchen will build a solid following in the years ahead, as will the happy little Havanese. The mighty little Jack Russell Terrier, long a very popular breed in this country and a fixture in stables and at horse shows but not heretofore recognized, had official recognition as of April 1, 2000. The Black-and-Tan Coonhound has long been the only one of the Southern coonhounds to have recognition, but the Plott Hound (they are both descended from the Bloodhound) will soon be attracting attention as well.

That leaves only two other breeds in the Miscellaneous Class, just about an all-time low—the Polish Lowland Sheepdog (called the Pons by its friends) and an Italian hunting dog that has been very popular in Europe, the Spinone Italiano.

If anyone is coming into the world of dogs, it might be fun to do it with a breed that is new to almost everyone. Imagine the thrill of being the first person ever to finish a Spinone Italiano and get it a UD (Utility Dog) obedience title as well. It would take a lot of hard work and it would be a bit of a long shot to get your name into the history books working with Poodles and Beagles, but you very well might do that with the Spinone Italiano or the Havanese or Canaan Dog. But first the breed must appeal to you. If it is a newly recognized or rare breed, so much the better. There is plenty of room for taste as well as a sense of adventure and exploration in the world of dogs. (Finding a major for the Spinone can be slow going!)

There Is
a Breed
for You

Chapter

4

P robably the most important decision would-be dog owners and exhibitors have to make concerns the breed selected: what breed is perfect, or nearly so, for the home they have to offer and the challenges they expect their dog to meet? No question is more important. It is all about building your family and focusing your love, not to mention committing to the considerable expenses involved. Like children, pets are an ongoing responsibility, and some are far more costly to keep than others. Still, love and personal satisfaction matter most. If you pick wisely and well, it almost won't matter that your friend doesn't go BIS every weekend.

There is a simple, commonsense process of elimination that can be helpful when deciding on a breed of dog. Three questions have to be answered by anyone seriously interested in having a dog, for show or not.

First, the practical consideration of size: (1) giant, (2) large, (3) medium, (4) small, or (5) wee. A 2- to 5-pound

Chihuahua and a 110-pound Scottish Deerhound may just be breeds within a single species (it could be hazardous or at least awkward, but they could be crossbred, perish the thought), but they do have their somewhat obvious differences.

Then, second, is coat care: (1) a great deal, (2) a minimal and reasonable amount, or (3) almost none at all. If the dog is going to be shown, his coat can be a huge consideration because of the attention a judge will pay to it in the ring. In some of the heavily coated breeds, few details matter as much.

A quick check of the standards shows the degree to which coat quality varies in importance. A Brussels Griffon's coat is worth twenty-five points of the one hundred points needed for perfection. A Lakeland Terrier's coat counts for fifteen points, a Sealyham Terrier's for ten. A Boston Terrier's and a Bulldog's coat are worth just two points. If you are battling to get your competitive partner as near to one hundred points as possible, it is of some considerable significance that, if you are showing a Brussels Griffon, the little guy's coat is mathematically worth twelve and a half times as much as it would be if you were showing a Boston Terrier.

Some people love all the primping and fussing that inevitably go with a beautifully coated dog, while others hate it. Taking care of a show coat requires a lot of time, infinite patience, space (many coated-dog owners allocate a special room, including a raised bathtub with a hand shower, to this single task; frequently a family room or garage has to do), some equipment (probably including a portable grooming table that can go to shows with you), and lots of cleaning up once the gussying up is done.

Dogs like the Poodles (Toy and Nonsporting Groups), Keeshond and Norwegian Elkhound (the former a Nonsporting, the latter a Hound—don't ask me why!), and herding dogs like the Bearded Collie don't require, they downright demand, constant care. That is a world unto itself. You love it or you hate it, but one way or another you have to provide it or your friend is going to look like a hoopoe's nest in no time flat. (The hoopoe, *Upupa epops*, has the dirtiest, messiest nest in just about all of birdom. From the point of view of style, that is easier to accept with *U. epops* than it is with His Worship the Poodle.) There is no place in the show ring for a bad-hair day. Clearly, coat has to be a factor in picking your breed.

The third factor in this preliminary elimination (and that is all this is) concerns exercise requirements. If the dog is to be kept in top condition and be happy, exercise is a requirement as critical as feeding. It is not just a small adjunct to daily maintenance. Either your dog is going to adjust his lifestyle to suit yours or you will have to do the same thing to suit his. An active dog is not going to be at his best in an inactive household. It is not easy to keep an Australian Shepherd or a Chesapeake Bay Retriever—or its owner—happy with his Frisbee when he has to pass underneath a grand piano and dodge several Spode jardinieres in order to make his catch.

Think of how wrong a new owner can go. Let us posit that the owner-to-be has a tendency to be sedentary and thinks of a quick trip to the nearest hydrant as high-impact aerobics. He owns a Jane Fonda workout tape to show him how he can get his dog and himself there and back. Nothing daunted, he gets a Border Collie, a breed that looks on twelve miles of running as a warm-up and likes to be extremely active from dawn until he falls off his legs long after dusk. Also, the owner has no land to speak of. He is a dedicated urban creature. His backpack comes from Gucci and so do his low-cut, laceless "hiking" boots. He doesn't even own a car. He has no means of getting his dog out into the countryside. It is probably a disaster in the making for man and dog alike. It is highly unlikely that this dog owner will have a flock of sheep. Border Collies are shepherds, and shepherd they will, one way or another. No sheep, they'll take grandchildren. No grandchildren available, they'll herd the washbasin, the bathtub, the hamper, and the commode. One Border Collie we heard about regularly puts all of the houseplants in the middle of the living room rug whenever he is left alone. He has to make things orderly and neat. What he herds doesn't matter very much. Not to suggest such dogs are not wonderful, but emotionally, they are anal as hell.

Another family lives in an urban apartment without any real likelihood of improving on the acreage situation in the near future. Despite that, the family gets a Mastiff or Bull-mastiff, ideal estate dogs, and everyone goes quietly insane together. Well, sometimes quietly and sometimes quite noisily. They are forever tripping over each other, becoming more bruised and claustrophobic by the minute. Sometimes guests have actually been injured. In these thundering encounters, the dog is innocent, just too big for the space allotted to it.

The underexercised dog is likely to become obese and increase its propensity to break wind. Breaking wind under such circumstances can tarnish your silver and stop your watch. You can always tell when it has happened—you get a vertigo attack, including double vision, or a migraine. Either way, the dog smiles. A bored dog, even if he is smiling, is likely to create an unsatisfactory condition in the home.

Another family has little spare time; both adults work, and they have limited discretionary funds for even routine professional grooming. They get a Bearded Collie or a Keeshond and gradually stop playing tennis and going to wine tastings. There is no longer any time for things like that. And eventually other outside activities involving extra funds are eroded.

The subject of conditioning can't be stressed too much. Snickers lives in a town house but gets constant work and play routines. She has plenty of time with a tennis ball and a Frisbee. That is not only healthy but also gives the dog quality time with members of her human family. Judges often comment on her solid body and excellent tone.

There are a number of different ways people take an interest in (fall in love with) a breed of dog. Rhonda, an incipient dog lover, came to the farm, fell in love with my Whippet, Topi (how could she not?), and decided that she had to have one, too. And along came Snickers. There is that way. People also fall in love with an exciting performance in a motion picture or on a television show: a Border Collie in *Down and Out in Beverly Hills* (that dog, Mike, was the sire of my Border Collie, Duncan); a Dalmatian, obviously, in *101 Dalmatians*; a Saint Bernard in *Beethoven*. There have been scores of others. Surely King and Rin Rin Tin had a great deal to do with the popularity of the German Shepherd, and Lassie helped elevate the Collie to tremendous heights. Publicity works for animals as well as it does for people.

And, too, there are fads, the *in* breeds, the-thing-to-do breeds—get a Komondor, for example. But be warned: Fads are not the way to go. They never have been. The dogs representing these breeds may be wonderful, generally, but when one comes to live with you, it is necessary for the two of you to suit each other in a number of different and often special ways. The relationship between you and your pet is not unlike a human friendship. You have other people in your life; your friend does, too. Yet, together, you two have something that is unlike any other combination on earth, something that is yours alone.

Avoid fads; they can lead to heartbreak. If everyone on the block has a particular breed of dog, surely you shouldn't get one, too. It is just plain common sense. If a breed is a fad, it is almost certainly being overbred, with the inevitable puppy-mill carelessness that entails disaster. It is quite possible to locate dangerous Labradors, stupid Goldens, and nasty examples of just about every breed. All you have to do is find some puppy-mill puppies in a pet shop and learn firsthand just how much bad breeding can do to fine dogs. Labradors, incidentally, are not dangerous, nor are Goldens witless, not unless they are bred that way.

So there we have some unavoidable considerations. If you have a hankering for a Saint Bernard, you may have to choose between that breed and a Porsche convertible. A Lotus would just not work out with a Newfoundland. A Rhodesian Ridgeback half crazed for the want of exercise can be a real downer in an apartment-house elevator when an elderly couple tries to join you in your descent. Here is where you must bring your powers of analysis into play. You all want to be supremely happy together, but the structure of the arrangement that will make that possible is the human partner's responsibility. The dog doesn't buy you. You are asking the dog to join your family. Whether you actually show your dog or not is not an issue here. Compatibility and comfort are. And you should never lose sight of that fact. Give the initial relationship a chance. The details of showing your dog, if such is your desire, will reveal themselves as you and your dog move along together. But before you move you have to bond.

In the final analysis, your choice will be essentially aesthetic. It will depend in large part on what you as an individual find beautiful, what you can't or at least don't want to live without. That is a very personal decision, obviously. What is so amazing is the variety of dogs available and what appeals to whom.

With few exceptions I find just about all dogs beautiful. I love their faces, especially their eyes; I love to watch them move and to interact with them on a one-on-one basis. There are relatively few breeds and random-bred dogs I wouldn't enjoy. In our forty-six years of marriage, my wife, Jill, and I have owned an awful lot of dogs, about sixty in all.

When it comes to purebred dogs, I do have a special place in my heart for a number of breeds: Whippets, West Highland White Terriers, Greyhounds, Bloodhounds, Great Danes, Jack Russell Terriers (recently recognized by the AKC and extremely popular with the horsy set and more and more so with urban folks in apartments; some of them can be real stinkers, but when they are nice, they are very, very nice). I love, too, Golden and Labrador Retrievers, Toy Poodles, Mastiffs and Bullmastiffs, Doberman Pinschers, Bassets, English Cocker Spaniels—and there are so many more. That doesn't mean that I like Standard Poodles or German Shepherds any the less, not really. It just means that I have owned and loved these other, special breeds myself or have known some personally and fallen for them. It will be the same for anyone seeking a dog for loving and showing. Novices should take their time. Let a naturally slow process unfold naturally. A bad or hasty choice or at least a careless one can mean a lot of sadness and wasted money. Picking the dog you are going to live with for the next ten to fifteen years is one of the few opportunities you will ever have to select a family member, besides your spouse. (Mordecai Siegal made that observation years ago.)

Before you say "Welcome to my heart," think it through. It really is quite an offer you have to make. One way or another the dog is going to repay you in kind, but his opportunity to do so will be provided by you.

Ouch! Biters

Although it isn't a major factor in the world of show dogs, there is a problem that occasionally raises its ugly head. Real dog people know that unfortunately there are breeds more inclined to resolve their frustrations with their teeth than other, more satisfactory companions are. That becomes an important factor if you have children living in your home or visiting there. The ultimate ostrich game is played by ignoring this problem. Oddly enough, good, dedicated breeders will usually be honest in a heart-to-heart talk about the biting propensity of their own breed. Promise them anonymity and listen to what they have to say with rapt attention.

There are several levels of or ways to define what are collectively and often mistakenly called dog bites. It is important to know these differences. The bottom level, the least damaging, evolves from the technique female wolves, and dogs as well, use to discipline their cubs or puppies. If a female is tired of the shenanigans displayed by one of her young, she may clamp her mouth shut, roll back her lips in a terrible snarl, and then really growl from deep down inside. It can be a most impressive display. The climax of this drama is an apparent lunge, as if to tear out the young animal's throat, but that is not the real intent, not at all. It is all show. The female in effect slaps or punches the youngster in a decidedly nonlethal way. Many so-called dog bites involving human victims are nothing more than that. A female, sick, hungry, tired, or just having an off day or week or year, punishes a pesky human kid with an incisor punch. No bite is intended, but teeth can be sharp and an accidental cut or abrasion is possible. But if there is no upper and lower part of the injury where the teeth clamped down, I question whether a bite was really intended or involved. A punch like that is still not desirable behavior. Damage can be done that can leave scars. It constitutes a breach of faith even if unintended. Of our resident eleven dogs, not one would even consider a bite or punch-bite. It is very simple; one of the earliest commands they learn here on the farm is: "No teeth!" or "No bite," even in play.

A word of warning: some bitchs are very nervous about young puppies they have borne. They would rather not have them handled. If you teach her there is no danger, she should let you handle them whenever you want to. All this is done while you are praising her. Go slow, offer no threat, recognize her sensitivities, and keep strangers, particularly kids, away from the puppies until everything is settled.

The second form of dog bite is just that, a bite by a dog. Fortunately, most occur on the extremities; there will be teeth marks on both sides of the hand or ankle. Clearly, whatever happened was intended. This is bad news for man and dog, and careful consideration has to be given as to whether the dog can stay in the family. There are trainers who specialize in aggressive dogs. They are very expensive (and rightfully so), but they are usually successful and are probably your only sensible choice. The sooner an expert takes over after an incident the better.

It can get quirky. The late, great film director Stanley Kubrick bumped into me in the then MGM studio, Elstree, north of London in Hertfordshire. He invited Jill and me to join the Kubrick clan for dinner that night. Coincidentally, he wanted to talk about dogs, creatures he dearly loved.

When we arrived, he gave me the background story while we had cocktails. He had bought a West Highland White Terrier for his three young daughters. The Westy is traditionally one of the sweetest dogs there is. In my whole life I have known only two cranky ones, and Stanley owned one of them. It had bitten him; his wife, Christiane; all three of their daughters; along with assorted aides, servants, delivery men, and service people.

I went to see the dragon in the kitchen, where he was napping in his bed under a small table.

"Hi there, Pup, what's the problem?" I asked, pulling up a chair slowly and being ever so soft and friendly. I was careful not to be threatening.

I made the hit list anyway. The *T. rex.* of dogdom with the nonstop cute face came out from under the table like a cruise missile with teeth painted on its warhead.

From what little I could see, this was one dog that wouldn't make it in a house with kids coming and going and sleeping over. With considerable reluctance I suggested that Stanley select a different breed or at least a different Westy from a different breeder. His problem would not lend itself to a quick or sure fix. The Kubrick dog had a screw loose.

But Stanley was a true dog lover and he went for a second opinion. He said that he wanted to give the dog every chance. He called the late lion tamer and circus owner Jimmy Chipperfield and told him the story he had told me. The Westy went off (in a Rolls Royce, as was only proper) for a brief stay with the Chipperfields. There the subject of biting could be given very careful attention. When the Westy with the teeth finally came home, he no longer bit like a spunky little frizzled-face terrier but like a lion instead. I didn't hear where the Westy finally landed, but his time terrorizing the Kubricks ended abruptly.

Jill and I had moved back to the United States when a letter from Stanley made it clear that an appropriate dog breed had to be found for life in an English manor house with walled grounds and a loving family. I recommended a Golden Retriever (they breed them superbly well in the United Kingdom). Stanley accepted the plan, and the last time I saw him he had three or four of them, all bouncing around him, rejoicing in their own life and his. Sadly, his is over. But he did love dogs.

Some Goldens do bite, it must be admitted, not many, but some. Most Westies do not, so what does this anecdote tell us? If you get your dog from a person you know and whose dogs you know, you will, in all probability, have an opportunity to meet at least one parent of the puppy you are considering. That doesn't necessarily prove anything, but you can get a pretty good indication of what your chances are for a sweet-dispositioned easy keeper. Do your research.

The third level of biting dog involves savaging instead of just biting. There has been a lot of that kind of thing reported in the news in the past few years. It is a very troublesome matter, and more than a few human deaths and a great many terrible mutilations have resulted from this ultimate level in intolerable canine behavior. It is rare that a healthy, well-bred, well-trained, and conditioned dog turns out to be a savage, but when it does happen, the owner will discover soon enough that showing is not really an option. There is no point to it; the individual dog in question should not be bred under any circumstances. A note in passing: Some of the sweetest dogs I have known have been Pit Bulls. When they are raised as pets and properly obedience trained, the kind of behavior we hear about and hate just doesn't become an issue. Breed-specific prejudice makes about as much sense in dogs as it does in people.

Some people, an awful lot perhaps, want a visual deterrent like a Doberman Pinscher or a German Shepherd, but the number of people who want a gregarious, responsive friend who is always reliable is far greater. It can be either of those two breeds or any other, but a dog, certainly a show dog, should be handleable even by strangers. It is a demand that is going to be repeatedly made of it in the show ring, and that is for certain. A dog that acts like a kite on the end of its leash just because a stranger approaches has as much chance of going Best in Show as I do of winning the Kentucky Derby afoot, carrying the horse.

There is a way that almost always seems to work in the evolution of a supernice dog, no matter what the breed. Handle him from the day he is whelped; have family members and friends handle him, too. Take turns carrying him around. Have him beside you when you read or watch television. Scratch him in all the good places and talk to him. The "good places" vary from dog to dog, but I find that a few inevitably elicit that glazed look of extreme pleasure. On the chest, between the front legs, is one, and another is lower down on the sides of the neck, from shoulder point to the lower jawline. On the back, at the base of the tail, a good scratching will often bring forth a reflexive kick or hunch-up. If you walk your dog often and find reasons to praise him, you will genuinely enjoy his company and he will rejoice in yours. Getting him to set up properly in the ring and move in keeping with his breed standards will be much easier if you two are a team with a history of interaction. It really isn't all that different from raising kids or being married. It is the story of giving and getting as played by two entities in goodwill for the pleasure of each. Rare is the dog that doesn't want to play that kind of game.

Setting up, or stacking, properly is a lovely thing to watch. That is when the dog looks his best. He has been trained to it and is doing it with the guidance of a thoroughly professional handler. While he is home he should practice stacking every day. Stack him on the floor if he is or is going to be large. Offer treats, make it fun. Practice walking with decorum on a lead, no more than five to ten minutes a day. Don't be a bore.

If his breed is normally shown on a table, practice that as well. Have strangers approach him and examine his body, his bite, his coat.

Go to matches; get him used to the ring, the judge's role, traveling; socialize at every opportunity. Be sure to make play part of his show experience. Keep the dog "up." A squeaky toy is a good thing to have in your pocket.

(Before going to a match where he can sniff around other dogs, make certain his shots are up-to-date. Check your plans with a veterinarian.)

A ring full of smart little terriers is one of the prettiest sights there is. Plucked and trimmed, in sparkling good health and coat, they are alert and snappy. I was watching a class of Lakeland Terriers years ago when all of a sudden, seemingly out of nowhere, a mouse appeared and shot across the ring. You will never see a smarter bunch of dogs. *Vermin!* The whole class went on full red alert. The mouse really had their attention. I don't know what eventually happened to the mouse, but that ring was clearly not the healthiest place for it to be. Long after it had vanished, the dogs were still rigidly alert and quivering.

Pick and

Choose

Chapter

5

Does Your Dog Look Like This?

GAY GLAZBROOK

WELSH TERRIER
Ch. Cisseldale's Radar

GREYHOUND
Ch. Gerico's Chasing the Wind

WEST HIGHLAND WHITE TERRIER
Ch. Mi 'Wee Perfect Impression

AMERICAN FOXHOUND
Ch. Kay-Phil's Lead On

BICHON FRISE
Ch. Paray's I Told You So

WHIPPET
DC Whippletrees Gold Nugget (Snickers)

BOXER
Ch. Carillon Elegance of Rummer Run

DOBERMAN PINSCHER
Ch. Telstar's Icon

LITTER OF DOBERMAN PINSCHER PUPPIES
Kaliber Dobermans

GAY GLAZBROOK

ENGLISH SETTER
Am/Can Ch. Blueprint Set'r Ridge's Zabri

GIANT SCHNAUZER
Ch. Skansen's Tristan II

PAPILLON
Am/Can Ch. Copper Mist Ice Dancer

Inevitably the question is asked, How much? What do high-quality puppies from really fine breeders cost, especially when they are mature enough to exhibit what appears to be show potential while still puppies? I have seen a Toy Poodle puppy sell for $10,000. Although that is admittedly high, the ten-month-old puppy was ultimately worth the price. The puppies she later produced were awesome, and her own show career proved to be very impressive. I have seen a Bulldog puppy sold for $2,500 and examples of lots of other breeds that went for between $250 and $300. There are a number of factors that are responsible for these widely divergent prices. If you are about to launch your dog-showing career, start with the very best puppy you can possibly afford. Try not to stint any more than your wallet absolutely mandates.

There are a number of questions that are inevitably

going to play a part when you set out to create the budget for your dream dog and its career:

1. Has the puppy started to show yet? Are there any points on record for it, or is it under six months? Does it appear to have real show potential? Is there a knowledgeable person who will go with you to visit the breeder? What does he think of your possible puppy? Try not to fall in love until the questions are answered and the results are in. There will be time enough to get goofy as the affair progresses.

2. What is the show record for the puppy's dam and sire? Are they both champions; how old were they before they finished (became champions)? How many champions have they produced in previous litters? How many Group Winners, how many Best in Shows? It is generally far easier to create a champion from champion stock, obviously. Don't be afraid of being snobby (just keep it to yourself). You are about to pick a team, cast a play, nominate a contender. There is one big difference: your dog is supposed to eventually be the foundation stock for your kennel name, and that was never so for quarterbacks, infielders, or presidential front-runners. But we do breed our dogs when the future needs their genes.

3. What is the puppy's genetic background when you go back further than its parents? Have there been ge-

netic diseases like displastic hips or progressive retinal atrophy? This can be all-important.

4. What does the puppy look like at this point? Is it al-
    ready a showstopper? Do people stop and try to en-
    gage you in conversation? If they don't now, they
    probably won't later. Do people ask you how much
    you want for the puppy? All good signs.

5. How about personality? Is it a reasonably assertive
    puppy not exhibiting undue shyness or timidity, or
    untoward aggression? Is it going to take on the show
    world with the same spirit Snickers has?

6. If the breed standards call for a specific color range
    or preferred markings, does the pup exhibit them?
    This can be a very important point, as with Dalma-
    tians, for example.

7. How is the puppy's present health? What kind of
    health records did its parents have? Is your choice
    bright-eyed, with a nice wet, cold nose and a healthy
    coat?

8. What is its breed? Is it a hard order to fill? Are there
    many quality puppies of that breed available? Since
    Bulldogs usually have one or perhaps two puppies, at
    most, and they are frequently born by Caesarean sec-
    tion, they can be quite expensive. That very large
    Bulldog head does not come without a price.

Anywhere between $250 and $10,000, and you should have your show dog to start out with. (In a lifetime of showing, you will probably never approach that higher figure. You will certainly edge up and well away from the lower.) Take extremely popular dogs like the Golden and Labrador Retrievers. They can be had for $300 to $900 ($1,000 to $1,250 for exceptional examples), but although they may be sensational companions, they are probably not going to look like examples of the same breeds that sell for $2,000 to $2,500, at least not prime examples. The difference between the $1,000 and the $2,500 puppies is in their predictable individual approaches to 100 percent of standard and the winning career of their parents and siblings from earlier litters.

There are additional factors in the price of a puppy.

1. How much does the breeder have invested in the parents?

2. What is the size and apparent quality of the rest of the litter?

3. What does the marketplace look like? How much in demand are puppies of this breed?

4. How badly does the breeder need money? (You probably won't ask.)

5. How badly do you want the puppy you have found? Are you consumed by the prospect of hugging it and

later its ribbons and trophies? How daffy will you allow yourself to get?

6. How does the breeder feel about you? This is not like a normal business dealing. The breeder wants to feel "comfortable" with your having a puppy. The breeder will want to know how much you will love it and how earnestly and therefore successfully you will show it. I have seen dogs go for both more and less than they should have because of this factor—the breeder's comfort zone. A sale very often launches new and lasting friendships.

A question often asked: Can a buyer have the puppy "vetted"—that is, examined by a veterinarian? Some breeders would treat such a suggestion with indignation, some would not. You guys will have to work that out between yourselves. One way to do it is to have a contractual return period. That could give you twenty-four to forty-eight hours to take the puppy to your veterinarian and check for discernible problems. Not a bad idea at all.

It is impossible to know in advance if you are going to be able to buy a puppy from a dam the quality of Snickers. There are just too many variables. Not until close to the end of the sixty-three-day gestation period is the number of puppies known—and then usually without absolute certainty. You don't know their actual number until they have all been whelped. It is not until months after that that the breeders know for sure how many promising show dogs there are in the litter. When that is known, the breeders have to decide how many, if any, they will keep for themselves and use to win more plaudits for their kennel name and how many they are going to be willing to sell.

Then comes the matter of who gets first pick. Breeders of fine dogs want their dogs shown well, again to enhance the kennel's reputation and because they love their breed. Well-known exhibitors who have shown dogs successfully over the years will usually be given first choice. Friends are accommodated, too, but most breeders are so serious about the puppies they produce that friendships are likely to come asunder before a potential champion gets into the wrong hands. Rarely if ever will breeders let any of their puppies, show quality or not, go into an irresponsible or substandard home, and then only by accident or misjudgment. The care that is taken is a combination of the love of their dogs, pride in their breeding, ego, possessiveness, a nurturing instinct, and a few other traits besides. Still, you have to start somewhere, and getting to know the right people at a show is usually the most productive first move.

Expect to be cross-examined and given both IQ and morality tests. It is best if your police rap sheet is very short and you don't have too many speeding tickets. It is very hard on the breeders to let their little darlings go. Never even try to get a puppy away from a breeder before it is eight weeks old. Many protectors of their breed prefer to wait longer than that. It can be months. It is always traumatic—but not for the poor benighted mother.

By the time one or two months of nursing is over, the bitch is ready to give all of her get (litter) away. Whether the litter is small or large, having those greedy little mouths with needlelike emerging teeth and those kneading paws with sharp little nails assaulting your naked abdomen is not fun after a few weeks. It is the pits. Not to mention that the wee critters are busy, when they are not nursing, eating their mother's tail and ears. By that stage most bitches think being a mother is the worst idea they ever had. You can watch the mother's patience wearing thin, thin enough so you can read through it. The fact that the puppies survive is a testament to what really nice animals dogs (bitches) really are.

One fact that seems to surprise most newcomers to the world of dogs is that the honest private breeder is simply trying to keep his losses to a minimum. The novice notes that the hobby exhibitor-breeder's Irish Setter has had a litter of eight puppies. There wasn't a stud fee involved, since the same breeder owned the sire as well, yet the breeder is asking a thousand dollars a puppy. In fact, there will be little if any profit. There rarely is. All the costs involved in traveling and showing the parents, creating your interest in their puppy because both of those parents became champions, have to be factored in, as do veterinary costs and all the elements of proper care of the dam, sire, and litter. Breeding fine show-quality puppies is rarely a reliable means of making money unless it is done on a thoroughly professional level with special facilities, kennel help, a groomer, handlers, the whole nine yards, including, in many cases, financial backers and co-owners.

The Truth about "Papers"

Although some dealers and pet-shop owners will tell you a different tale, a prospective pet's "papers" are meant to be free; they should not add to the price of the dog. In one case I was asked to look into, a pet shop sold an innocent first-time purebred dog owner a Bulldog at slightly over twice its fair market value and then offered "all the dog's papers" for an extra two hundred dollars. The buyer said that he was assured that it was a good deal—by the pet-shop dealer, of course. It was in fact a terrific deal—for the thieving merchant.

Keep in mind the following considerations regarding a dog's papers and other information acquired at time of purchase:

1. A pedigree is simply a list of a dog's forebears. Blank family trees or pedigree forms are available from dog-food companies, in books and magazines, just about everywhere you look in the dog world. Almost inevitably they are handouts, freebies. Fancy pedigree forms on parchmentlike paper with lots of scrolling are for sale from vendors at dog shows for almost no money at all. A pedigree lists the parents of the dog, grandparents, and great-grandparents at least—some-

times going much further back than that—by each dog's registered name and its AKC registration number. Computer printouts are generally available today. Do not do business with anyone who suggests a price for the pedigree or who appears reluctant to supply a free copy with the dog he is trying to sell you. It should be available at the time of the sale.

As a rule, I would suggest that you avoid anyone who is trying to sell you a dog. Fine breeders have to be begged to let go of one of their charges. It is like giving up their children. Be on the lookout for hustlers. There are plenty around. And it is not necessarily a minor backyard business. The American Society for the Prevention of Cruelty to Animals investigated one puppy-mill operation in Lancaster County, Pennsylvania, that averages close to a quarter of a million dollars a year supplying poorly bred, substandard dogs to pet shops. Some cottage industry! Some way to treat man's best friend!

2. When you buy a dog that is represented by the seller as eligible for AKC registration, you are entitled to receive at the time of sale an AKC application form properly filled out and signed by the seller. When you have completed your part, it is to be submitted to the AKC with a ten-dollar registration fee. When the AKC has processed the paperwork, you will receive a registration certificate. The seller should not

profit from this process, despite what some of them will tell you.

3. DO NOT buy a dog from a seller who is unable to submit to you all identifying information at the time of the sale. DO NOT accept a promise of later identification. Chances are you will never get what is properly yours, and you may never be able to show your dog or study its lineage, should the time and reason come when you want to breed it. Again, unless your purebred dog is of show quality and has what its breed needs, do not breed it. Spay or neuter instead. Never even think of breeding a random-bred or pet-quality purebred dog. Just love it. You will be getting more than your money's worth. Ribbons and trophies get tacked up in the kennel or tack room; the dogs themselves are for eternal hugging. They know it and if you don't, you will be missing an awful lot in life.

4. AKC rules require a seller to provide the buyer with a properly completed registration certificate including the breed, sex, and color of the dog, its date of birth, the registered names of the dog's sire and dam, and the name of the breeder. Stand firm, get what is yours, and briskly walk away from anyone who tries to put a price on a dog's papers. He probably sells snake oil, too.

5. Although not technically a part of registration papers, sellers should be able (and willing) to supply the buyer with a free copy of the dog's medical history outlining what shots it has had and what shots are due and when. It should contain all of the information the dog's future veterinarian will need. This can be terribly important. This information should be free; any other suggested arrangement is a hustle. Any true dog lover will be anxious for you to have this paper because it will help you and your veterinarian keep the dog they supposedly love healthy and happy.

6. The seller should also supply complete information on the dog's diet. Brand names, quantities, treats, feeding times, should all be included. Shortly after the new puppy (usually) comes home, you should discuss this paper and the medical record with your veterinarian, your dog's personal doctor.

It is the responsibility of a dog's buyer to get all of the paperwork and registration information required, and if it is not made available without cost, pass on the deal. Something is amiss in Denmark and probably elsewhere. That can be difficult to do, but in the long run it is far better for the animal and for your bank account.

A NAME FOR THOSE PAPERS

If you are buying a puppy, it probably will not have been individually registered with the AKC before you came along, so part of the information you will be submitting with your ten dollars will be your pet's official name. You can call your pet whatever you want at home, but Toots and Babe, Spot, Felix, and Phydeaux are not ring names. On the other hand, you might feel a little silly on the street where you live calling loudly, "Here Nightingale's Salmon Bracket Tester, come!" You need, then, a registered name, although you can forget it if you want, once it has become a part of canine history. If your dog's originating kennel is renowned for the quality of its puppies and their show performance, you may want to capitalize on that fact and use the kennel's name as part of your pup's registered name: Glorious Household's Shin Plaster Dandy, for example. But hold on, you can't, unless you have written consent. You must get that consent at the time of the purchase in writing from Glorious Household Kennels. It generally is a good sign if the kennel gives you that permission. It means the kennel feels strongly enough about the potential of the puppy they have bred to want it out there attracting attention to their presumably good name. If a kennel refuses, it may be because they have a policy that mandates that position or they feel your pup is a pet-quality dog *or* they do not feel you will do a good job of showing the puppy they have sold you. Either way, it is the buyer's job to ask for permission.

A word or two about those fingernail-on-the-blackboard

poofy names: the whole idea is to come up with something new. After all, the AKC registers more than a million dogs a year, every year, and even with the dog's abbreviated life span, there are going to be a lot of registered dogs still alive at the same time. Millions! No two can have the same name. Now, go forward and invent. If you can come up with a new name for a Golden Retriever with *gold* in it not currently occupied you are very inventive indeed. A lot of breeders have a sense of humor, and since the name won't be used very much in real life anyway, they like to come up with puns and plays on words. Sometimes it is just quirky. Jill produced a litter of Bloodhounds and called it her J litter; all the puppies had names beginning with that letter— Jasmine, Jeremy, Jethro, and so on. Anyway, show dogs are not generally called Babe or Bo, Mabel, Maud, or Musty, except at home.

After Your Puppy Comes Home

So, then, you have at last found your breed, you have located and perhaps befriended your breeder, and you know what you want the incoming member of your family to accomplish. What is more important, you have identified your pick-of-the-litter puppy and you are anxious to get his career under way. It is time to stop dreaming, time to make the dreams come true. What are the next steps?

Take your puppy, as soon as possible, to your veterinarian, his personal doctor. Tell the seller you are going to do that as soon as you leave and have the understanding that your veterinarian's word will be the deciding vote. No one should object to that. Have him checked out and establish a schedule for his immunizations. Good health comes first. Don't try to go anywhere without it. It won't happen. A dog that is in anything short of perfect health just won't show well. The judge will spot it immediately.

Manners comes next. Check into an obedience course as soon as the professional you have decided to confer with says it is time. Learn to work together as a team. Everything will be easier after that. This isn't a matter of turning your companion into a robot. Rolling over and playing dead is not what it is all about; it is about instilling good manners and encouraging obedience. *Come, sit, stay, down, off, no* or *leave it, give it up,* or *drop it:* these commands are not too much to expect of a bright puppy that is well cared for, encouraged and socialized, and properly rewarded. Many people feel you should not teach a puppy to sit until it is more than a year old and familiar with showing. In the ring, a *come* is followed by a self-stack, not a sit. Either way he will do much better in the ring with obedience training. Praise him, then praise him again. He will play your game with you—and for you—but he wants to be recognized and rewarded. He may not be exactly certain what it is all about, but he knows it can be exciting, it pleases you, and there are rewards. He knows praise when he hears it and he can never get enough of it. It is addictive.

Even before he starts showing, your new friend should

rehearse! Setting up—holding the show stance as he is supposed to when the judge evaluates his qualities—is an easy lesson, something you can do together that will give him a head start when he does finally get launched as a show puppy. He should know how you want him to relate to his leash and how you want him to move.

And the business of being handled: few things are more important. The puppy should react well to strangers. He should not be suspicious or shy or nervous, against the day when the judge's hands will examine his body. The touch of a stranger should not appear dangerous or threatening, and a well-conditioned show dog knows that. If he doesn't, it does not bode well for future competition. A judge pressing down on his withers, checking how his upper and lower jaws sit opposite each other, spot checking his maleness, running hands along his back and down his sides: not dangerous, not unpleasant, and it is essential that the pup understand this perfectly well. A squirming dog or, heaven forbid, a biting one probably won't have far to go in his career.

There is one thing about touch that can be a little confusing. When a male dog is being evaluated, you will note the judge perform a fast darting ritual between the dog's rear legs. The judge (some do this with a shy grin, others with a slightly grim, stern look) is checking to be certain that both of the dog's testicles have descended into the scrotum. (You get to talk about these things with ease when you are into dogs.) If the two are not there to be counted, if there is only one apparent, the dog is called a monorchid and will have to be disqualified. I have watched judges do this little examination scores of times, very often on dogs that are already champions and presumably have been checked scores of times before. Where do they think the testicles have gone? Perhaps they come and go at will, rather like Mr. Otis's invention. Bitches don't have to worry about things like this. It is not an indignity they are expected to suffer. (Of course, if a bitch has had a litter recently and has been nursing, she may have to walk around wearing a tight T-shirt or a tightly wrapped bandanna as an extended belly band. Her owners are trying to get her breasts to shrink and give her back her girlish figure. No one wants to see a show bitch waddling around with a pendulous belly like teatime at Romulus and Remus's house.)

Back to testicles for a moment (a line we don't get to use very often). The story is often told of an otherwise beautiful Boxer specimen, I think it was, with only one descended testicle. The owner talked a veterinarian into inserting an artificial one made of rubber to make things seem right. By the rules of the show ring that is a no-no, big time. Physical faults should not be altered for show purposes. They got away with it for a time, but then the second testicle descended, as can happen. The next time out, the judge shot his hand to the target, then turned to the handler with a puzzled look.

"Three?"

Trials

and Then

Some

Chapter

6

Obedience Trials

The dog "show" second in popularity only to the standard conformation show is the obedience trial. The AKC either licenses or sanctions the trial, and it can be appended to a conformation show or staged as a separate event unto itself. (A member trial is an event staged by a club that is an AKC member; a licensed trial is staged by a club that generally is not an AKC member; and a sanctioned trial is an informal event where titles are not earned. It is a kind of tailgate picnic with dogs. And a fine time is had by all.) The AKC licenses or sanctions twenty-two hundred or more such contests a year.

In the obedience trials, handler and animal are judged together as a team, with one member highly responsive to the other. Breed standards play no role and the events are not breed specific. Anybody can compete against anybody. Even spayed and neutered dogs can participate without prejudice. It is a case of performance, not beauty, although many participants have earned conformation championships in their careers as well. Beauty and brains are by no means mutually exclusive. It is simply a matter of what ranks highest in the owner's and perhaps the dog's "opinion," if it does come down to a choice between the two. Much of what the dog accomplishes is strictly a function of the time, effort, and training on the part of the owner or handler.

Think of obedience as a very challenging second show career, a valued backup should a planned show dog's career not work out in conformation. An outsize feature, a late-developing undershot or overshot jaw—these things don't matter when the subject is exclusively brains and performance. If a dog can't make it in the world of conformation for one reason or another, it can still go on to be recognized as the best obedience dog in town. That is no small accomplishment. By no means are obedience trials for would-bes or any other second-stringers. Obedience titles are hard earned, highly respected, and sources of great pride for the owners. They can add mightily to the value of a dog and its offspring. They are also great fun for man and beast and are wonderful bond tighteners. They make any dog much, much easier to live with. Obedience fosters a kind of man-dog brotherhood and profoundly affects the way dog and partner get along together.

There are three levels in obedience judging. Each has a set routine of exercises for the judge to score, and they become progressively more complex as the team advances.

Winning at the Novice level can earn your dog the title CD for Companion Dog. Next is Open, with the title CDX, for Companion Dog Excellent. The highest level is Utility, UD, for Utility Dog. Relatively few dogs in the general population, even show dogs, come near any one of these higher titles in their deportment unless they have been meticulously trained to the task. The world would be a much better place if that weren't so! (That would be true of kids, too.)

The six exercises in Novice, the first level, are what any well-brought-up companion dog should know and do as a matter of course. No canine rocket science required here, just the ability and the desire to work closely with a human partner and accept graciously the praise that comes with success.

The six Novice exercises are:

1. heel on a leash,

2. stand for examination (where the handler poses his dog off-lead for a brief examination by the judge— the form of the pose is the handler's option),

3. heel free (off-lead),

4. recall (where the dog remains where and as his handler left him until recalled),

5. long sit (one minute), and

6. long down (three minutes).

These commands are typically obeyed with enthusiasm and the same inherent sense of showmanship exhibited by any good show dog and companion. The obedience ring is not the place for laid-back, lackadaisical dogs. It is a place for pizzazz and excitement. It is a crowd pleaser for the people who understand what they are looking at. Wonderfully intelligent dogs trying so hard to please their human partners have a beauty all their own. In a very real way it is what sharing your life with a dog is all about. We have been at it for at least 150 to 200 centuries. We should be good at it. So should the dogs, and they generally are.

The Open schedule adds extra elements: (1) drop on recall, (2) retrieve on flat, (3) retrieve over high jump, and (4) broad jump. The Utility requirements add still others: (1) signal exercise, (2) two scent discrimination tests, (3) directed retrieve, (4) directed jumping, and (5) group examination.

A dog earns his obedience title when he scores 170 points out of an ideal 200 in that "leg" and gets more than 50 percent of the points for each exercise. Although the exercises are different in each of the three legs, the numbers— 170 out of 200 and 50 percent—remain the same. A dog can go on for his Obedience Trial Championship only after receiving his UD, Utility Dog, title. For his championship, a dog must earn 100 points that include a first place in Utility with at least three dogs in competition and a first place in Open with at least six dogs in the competition and a further first place in either of these competitions. The three firsts

A Parenthetic Word about Ownership

An increasingly large number of people strenuously object to the use of the words *owner* and *ownership* when speaking of dogs because of the arrogant mind-set that is behind them. Undeniably there is a bit of bra burning in that, but there is also some logic and certainly some morality. "People don't *own* animals, certainly not companion animals," these people argue. "People and animals own each other in a very real sense; it should be a reciprocal affair, a partnership in every sense of the word." This semantic exercise wouldn't be all that important, perhaps, if people didn't act like they were owners and if so many people didn't overlook their responsibilities and do things that are out-and-out cruel, careless, and, ah, well, stupid. If people didn't have the superior attitude that often seems to go with being an owner and thought of themselves rather as partners in the relationships they help foster, things might go a lot better for the dogs we have in our families. It certainly happens that way with husbands and wives, parents and kids. There is more than political correctness to this issue; it's a lot about love and respect and giving as good as you get. Personally, I go along with it. I think of my dogs (and cats, and horses and other hoofed critters, and one supersweet cockatoo) as friends rather than property. I hate the idea of having dominion over other lives. I didn't ask for it and I am not proud of it. Yet, as it turns out, it is an essential part of having these animals in my life and of my being a part of theirs.

129

must be under three different judges. A championship in obedience is an enormous accomplishment. And the necessary skills remain with the dog for as long as it lives. Obedience champions are generally the best of all canine citizens. You can tell. There is a spring in their step. Their handler's step, too.

There is a certain panache about a successful obedience dog, a distinctive way it relates to its owner and the world around it. It seems to understand the world better than most dogs and enjoy itself in special ways. People typically react to these accomplished companions with more respect. They are special dogs and obviously they have had a lot of quality time with their owners. That is a given. Many people prefer obedience competition to conformation and make a championship in that part of showing a dog their primary goal. The dogs seem to love it, perhaps because it is all about them and what they can do.

Field Trials

Four categories of field trials are sanctioned by the AKC: Hounds, pairs (braces) or packs in pursuit of hare and the cottontail rabbit (started as a formal competition in 1890); Pointing (since 1874); Retrieving (instituted as a field trial in 1931); English Springer Spaniel, for the old Spaniel game of flushing (since 1924). Cocker Spaniels and English Cocker Spaniels are no longer used in this part of the game. They have been assigned other duties: full-time love, the giving and getting thereof. Their position in the Sporting Group today is simply a matter of tradition, of which the dog-show world has a great many.

I, for one, would be unrelentingly opposed to the Hound events where live rabbits and hare are used, if the target or quarry animals were harmed. The AKC has assured me that they are never touched, and Dr. Steven Zawistowski, senior vice president of The American Society for the Prevention of Cruelty to Animals, the "A," and a big Beagle man, has participated as judge, breeder, exhibitor, and steward, and in other capacities, in more than a thousand of these trials and has never seen a rabbit harmed. Based on the AKC denial that harm is done and Dr. Zawistowski's testimony corroborating that, I accept things as I have been assured they are. No test, trial, or show in any category could justify harming other animals.

For a lot of people, understandably, these trials are not what companion dogs are all about. Obedience is much more to the point. Conformation is a given. Pride of ownership suffuses all, that and the joy of competition. Both human and canine participants can find what they want in dog shows. Not everyone wants the same things, but there is plenty of sport and hubris there for everyone.

There is such a lineup of performance competitions (field trials, herding contests, lure coursing trials) that there are actually thirty-nine titles a dog can earn besides Ch. for Champion. Unless you have a special interest before you decide to show dogs, you probably won't be looking for OA

(Open Agility), MH (Master Hunter), NAFC (National Amateur Field Champion), or JE (Junior Earthdog). You can show dogs for the rest of your life and never even know that such an alphabet soup exists. To the people who do pursue other doggy interests besides conformance, these other competitions are all-important and very exciting. The dogs are always special, and the pride and the joy of the owners are boundless.

Among the special areas (breeds) of interest in the Hound category are the Basset Hounds. In field trials Bassets are judged for searching ability, pursuing ability, accuracy in trailing, proper use of voice (proclaiming all finds and denoting progress without being noisy, silly, or overly talkative), endurance, adaptability, patience, determination, independence, cooperation, competitive spirit, and intelligence. Faulty performances are listed as quitting, backtracking, ghost trailing (chasing a trail that doesn't exist), pottering, babbling, swinging, skirting, leaving checks, running mute, tightness of mouth, racing, running hit or miss, lack of independence, and bounding off. That is a long list of dos and don'ts and it explains why people with Basset Hounds think of them as very special dogs. In fact it is difficult to argue any other view. Bassets are special, very. If nothing else, our Bassets make us laugh. It can be difficult to think of them as serious trail dogs, but that is what they are. They take themselves seriously and expect you to, too.

The lures used in Basset Hound field trials are rabbit and hare. Again, the AKC and experienced participants swear the animals are never harmed and I have no information to the contrary. Insofar as it is true, these contests are wonderful sporting events. The trials are run in appropriate countryside: fields, meadows, marshes, woodlands. The same dogs can be in conformation shows as well, and there are beautiful examples of western European hunting dogs to be seen. *Basset*, in French, means low to the ground. Obviously, they are. And they have the most glorious voices. They're special.

Dachshunds and twenty Terrier breeds are eligible to participate in Earthdog tests. Dogs that are spayed or neutered may join in the fun, as can the Jack Russell Terrier, which has just become a recognized breed.

Most people don't realize that couch potatoes like Westies and Dachshunds and Miniature Schnauzers (aka lap dogs) can participate in the rough-and-tumble world of field trials, including Earthdog tests. Well, they can. There is something for almost everybody in the amazing world of dogs in competition.

The quarry in these trials are rats in cages. Here, again, the quarry are not harmed, although it probably is not what the rats would most like to do on a brisk Saturday morning. (We are not generally nice to rats on Saturday morning or any other day of the week. They have had very bad press.) One supposes that they are not volunteers in these contests but are shanghaied with relatively little formality. There are AKC regulations that require the caged critters to be fed and watered. The dogs, too, of course, are fed and watered. It is optional only in the case of handlers and judges. They can take care of themselves.

The dens where the competitors go to ground are, in the case of Junior Earthdog testing, at the end of thirty-foot tunnels with three ninety-degree turns. The dog, released ten feet from the tunnel entrance, has thirty seconds to reach the quarry. It can receive no instructions during the hunt or it is disqualified. The energy expended in the game is boundless and includes a lot of barking. These are noisy, exciting little hunters.

Senior Earthdogs have to tackle tunnels with a blind (false) den and a false exit. They, too, race against the clock. The attitude the Earthdogs exhibit is positively volcanic: quarrelsome and fairly bursting with energy and enthusiasm. They take it all very seriously. Digging furiously after vermin is what they were bred to do.

Stamina Can Help You Survive

Many dogs exhibit a great deal of enthusiasm and it is a good idea to match your own physical resources—bodily strength and agility—to the task to which you are putting your dog if you are doing the handling yourself. There can be a lot more to owning a dog than brushing, trimming, and tossing the odd Frisbee now and then. The enthusiasm a dog shows is a measure of the regard he has for you. He wants to please you, to be praised and rewarded. As for you, survive it. If you are well suited to arm-wrestle an Affenpinscher, think twice before availing yourself of a Komondor or a Great Pyrenees.

Jane, a regular at dog shows, had a misadventure that wasn't the direct outcome of a competition, but it does show the power dogs can exhibit when they are baited by life itself. And Jane's mishap did occur at a dog show, after all.

Jane had been successfully showing her champion Bloodhound, Luke, a magnificent slobber-chops moose of a dog. Jane was a stunningly beautiful woman who always dressed to the nines. There was only one grievous fault in her style—she wore acres and acres of furs, real ones (a very unfeeling thing to do around dogs, I think, even if they get to keep their furs on their own backsides, at least in this country). On this particular day, a bright fall day with the trees around the show grounds in Washington, D.C., showing off their best foliage, Jane was wearing a double-breasted, full-length mink, part of what she thought of, erringly, as her own best foliage. As lovely as she was, that is how offensive her coat was. Even people who liked her, and most people did, hissed at her coat. She was oblivious. She just didn't get it.

If you have never handled a Bloodhound, be advised that performance on the front end of a lead is not generally their strongest suit. They lunge and pull ferociously, although they are otherwise generally the sweetest of dogs, and I have never known one of this breed to be anything like ferocious. The point is that they have been bred to lead you, not follow you. After all, in pursuit of a lost camper, a child, or an escaped desperado, you are not the one out front on all fours sniffing. That would be patently absurd. One has to be alert. Jane, in all her finery, was not, although she should have known better. Luke was a fun-loving dog with the strength of a bull and a bear combined.

Something absolutely irresistible crossed paths with Luke's incredible nose (it is rumored that it was a cat), a nose estimated to be about two million times as sensitive as our snubby little counterparts. Jane stretched straight out behind Luke like a kite in a Chinatown parade, making excited little yipping sounds, but she held on to the leash as if releasing it would plunge her into the depths. (It would have.) Luke bounded off, dragging poor Jane face down behind him, flopping around and now making helpless little gasping and gurgling sounds. She said something vaguely like *helpppppppp*, poor dear.

Right across the show grounds Luke went, never looking back and not minding the dead weight dragging on the ground just a leash away. He dashed across an area of cement with Jane still grimly holding the lead. By the time Jane was rescued and Luke arrested in his flight, Jane, staggering to her feet, yelped something about her mink having gone bald. Not only that, having been unable to control where she was going, she had managed, at the tail end of Luke's parade, to adorn her shorn coat with that which one expects to find where hundreds and hundreds of dog are gathered. She and her coat were a dreadful mess. Luke, as Bloodhounds are likely to do in situations like this, wagged his tail, yawned, and, of course, drooled. No one wished Jane harm, anything but; however, the folks who were on hand wept not for the fur.

So, there is that consideration: physical limitations on your part. The different breeds have very different styles, and some are good at some things and not at others. A full day at a dog show, as we suggested earlier, can be tiring, to understate things to a British degree. Even wee little dogs that can't turn you into a kite still require carrying and grooming, and there is also a box of their gear to handle. With grooming table and all, a ten-pound dog can require forty pounds of gear, while a Great Dane that weighs in at more than one hundred pounds can have all its grooming needs in a first grader's lunch box.

While you are planning your dog's show career, and to ease the burden on your own stamina, you might want to seriously consider a professional handler. Their fees are reasonable and they can do an awful lot for your dog's career. (One supposes that paid handlers can be used in any competition where the AKC does not prohibit them. One normally associates them with conformation shows, however, not trials.)

If you want to be there for the fun and excitement, by all means tag along. Your dog will be comforted with you near at hand. Perhaps, since he probably lives with you (ours always did), you can urge him along and give him confidence. His needs are comparable to those of his human counterparts. We don't know how or what dogs think, but there is some mechanism in there that insists that dogs do think and participate with palpable glee. Your presence adds to all of that.

Professional dog handlers who work full-time at the game can provide you with the advice you are going to need if you and your dog are climbing aboard. They are known to the judges and know which judge is most apt to give your offering a second and perhaps favorable look. There are those matters of style and taste. People long exposed to the wonder of the dog-show world can tell you which handlers are best known for which type or group of dogs. If you get a well-known handler, fair or not, your dog will have an edge in the ring. That is just the way it is. The dog will be shown to advantage, and some judges hold some professional handlers in such esteem that they are not unwilling to question their own taste in dogs. They know no handler wants to handle less than wonderful dogs. There are judgment calls there, and lots and lots of skill. A professional handler raises the ante a bit, but no one shows dogs so they can lose. Ask your breeder; he will know the best handler for you and the product of his breeding selections.

Meet the "Competition"

Who does these things to themselves? Whether it be a conformation show, obedience trial, or field trial, dog shows have been described as self-inflicted wounds. Millions and millions of people live with and love their dogs, after all, but relatively few—a few hundreds of thousands—really submerge themselves in so demanding a sport. In case you hadn't noticed, horsey people talk mostly about horses and doggy folk can match them any time talking mostly about their dogs. Both species are all-consuming passions. The human players act as if they were mesmerized by the game. (They are.) It becomes compulsive behavior and an ongoing lesson in geography, since in the course of a year's showing an exhibitor will end up in cities he has barely heard of before. Some of the best-traveled folks around are dog-show enthusiasts. A well-known oral surgeon I know has been invited to Australia, Hungary, and many other countries to judge the Sporting Group.

There are good people and bad people to gossip about at dog shows; the good people are always referred to by either their first names or their first and last names run together as if they were all one name. In the case of people you think are bad, the last name is used. Gossip in the dog world enriches your time on the show grounds or in the arena. Besides brushing, grooming, and giving your dog exercise, there isn't a lot to do when you are not actually showing off your companion.

What do dog-show people have in common? First and I hope foremost is their love of dogs. For a small percentage of the people showing dogs, some kind of hubris comes first, but that is not usually the case. Some show dogs (a small percentage) don't even live at home. They live with, sometimes in the kennel of, the handler and never come to know the people who write the checks. Most show dogs, however, are pets in the finest sense of the word. In those cases where a show dog is a valuable "thing" and not a true pet, it is usual for it to bond with the handler with whom it spends just about all its time, not its actual "owner." It is not unusual for the true owner to give the dog to the handler as a gift when it finishes with its show career. I will confess it is a form or kind of dog loving that I fail to understand.

Almost universally, dog-show enthusiasts are dog lovers. A second universal characteristic is competitiveness. Winning is what it is all about. But I asked two ardent dog-show enthusiasts what was in it for them. Why their own deep involvement? My asking wasn't the first time they had thought about it.

Fred and Duffy have a whole life of involvements. They raised two daughters; Fred is a doctor with a very prestigious appointment; they have a lot of friends. They sail on their own boat. Both Fred and Duffy were raised with dogs and truly love them. Somehow, the dog-show thing moved in on Fred and he began going to shows whenever they were in his part of the world, just for the fun of watching. Next step, he began stewarding. He kept at it until he was spending half of the weekends in the year at this nonpaying job, keeping things moving along for the judge. He was learning about dogs and dog breeds at every show he attended—he still is learning, reads everything that comes his way, and never stops asking questions. He was talking dogs with exhibitors, judges, and handlers. He looked forward with eager anticipation to his very doggy weekends. Before long, of course, Duffy was deep into dog shows, too. Together with Connor the Westie, they pursue ribbons and titles weekend after weekend as if they were the pharaoh's treasure. Well, in a sense, they are. Anubis, you know.

Then, naturally, Fred had a canine addiction. He and Duffy have shown Old English Sheepdogs and West Highland White Terriers and are in the constant state of near euphoria that their hobby gives them. They sit at a cocktail reception with their Westie on Fred's lap. (The Sheepdog *en* lap would be unthinkable. Not only are they the size of ponies, their face is always wet.)

"Fred," I asked, "what is it about dog shows? What attracted you in the beginning and what holds you now? You are at one show or another at least half of all weekends in the year."

"First, there are the dogs. I love them. They fascinate me. I love to watch them work. Then there are the people."

"Can you find common denominators that define or at least describe this peculiar form of human animal?"

"They love dogs, too, and we certainly have that in common. I tend to like them, I enjoy their company and their enthusiasm. Even when we are not showing, I enjoy dogs and dog people. They are usually competitive, they like winning, but most of them are happy for you when you are winning. It is a generous corner of the world. They understand me and I understand them; we have so much in common. There is a lot of laughter at dog shows; dog people tend to have a sense of humor. They are usually hospitable and helpful.

"A novice exhibitor I know was showing an Old English Sheepdog at the beginning of her career. She was initially in way over her head. A couple of old-timers, real pros, went over to help her, help her increase the chances for a ribbon even though it was a dog they would soon be in contention with. That is real sportsmanship.

"I remember a case when a real amateur was getting ready to handle her dog in the ring for the first time. She was in a terrible flap. She had a heavy coat to contend with, and she knew too little about the tricks in the ring, where every trick is vital to success. Again some old experienced hands chipped in and got both her and her dog settled into the routine. She took a red ribbon.

"I have made a lot of friends and have met some wonderful people at dog shows. I treasure the whole experience."

Fred's points are well taken. There is camaraderie at dog shows and, inevitably, among the dogs themselves. That is a great combination. Serious complaining or actual fighting is rare. As long as short leashes are used and not allowed to become tangled, there are times when the dogs get along better than the people.

This "brotherhood" or "sisterhood," as the case may be, shows itself in many ways. A handler finds himself with a conflict, two dogs showing at the same time in two different rings. That happens very often.

He hands one of the leads off to another handler who is

free for the next class, and he can be satisfied that the dog will get a good showing. Another handler has his clippers break down and he has a dog to get ready for judgment day—borrowing the needed equipment, no problem. Cooperation is expected in picking up a dog to take to the show or dropping it off after the show, depending on load and timing, and that can save the dog's actual handler literally hundreds of miles of driving. The next time it will be his turn to pitch in and help.

There are just plain bad or stupid people in every field, and unfortunately dog shows are not the exception. Some years ago in New Jersey, it was a blisteringly hot day—really too hot for a show but, of course, the show went on as scheduled.

There were a number of cases of heatstroke (dogs *and* people). Some of each ended up in ambulances. One exhibitor or visitor locked his Boxer in his car without leaving the windows ajar. If he had left them wide open it probably wouldn't have been sufficient. A group of people gathered around the car and tried to get the doors open. No luck. One woman headed off to get the jack handle from her car; the idea of smashing the windshield had universal approval. A man ran over to the announcer's table and grabbed the microphone.

"Whoever the idiot is who locked a Boxer in a blue station wagon with Pennsylvania plates, your dog is nearly dead and you are about to lose all the glass in your wagon."

I don't know which thought galvanized the dog's owner,

the severely distressed dog or the imagined sound of tinkling glass, but a very shaky-looking man had to run the gauntlet to get to his car. There was a lot of name calling as he passed clusters of dog lovers, trying his best not to make eye contact with the gathered witnesses. He was told to leave the show grounds.

. The point, obviously, was the way people went into action when someone else's dog was in trouble. A dog is a dog is a dog, and the same thing is true of dog lovers.

Coming
and Going

Chapter

7

M any people, depending on the breed they have chosen, use the family car for transportation to and from the shows they attend. That is fine if you have a Boston Terrier, an Affenpinscher, or a Pug, but what about the likes of the Great Dane, Newfoundland, and Irish Wolfhound? More often these exhibitors have a "rig." It is not exactly clear what a rig actually is or should be except comfortable, safe, and convenient. (Forget miles-to-a-gallon—this is not the economic part.) Minimum wheels would be a station wagon, and it goes up from there—a drag-it-along-behind-you trailer, a pickup truck with a cap, a motor home, a camper, or any customized version of some or all of the above. I have seen dogs arrive in taxis and stretch limousines. One couple I know has a customized motor home that cost more than $165,000. Now, that is a jolly, comfortable rig! No dog should be ashamed to be seen traveling in that style. The trick is to keep your dog from expecting the limo.

They are usually quite willing to consider that their right. That can be the beginning of an attitude problem.

With a few exceptions, people do generally drive something to the shows. The alternatives to the highway are not all that promising: trains are largely impossible; the most likely of the available means is air transport. That can be a terrible idea unless you are prepared to take precautionary steps.

There can be very high risks in flying dogs to shows, or anywhere else, for that matter. If it is a day like that hot one in New Jersey years ago, it is extremely hazardous. A dog crate left on a loading dock with the sun pouring in probably bodes an oft-reported scenario: baggage handlers at the cold-drink machine and one asphyxiated dog in the sun. Cold weather can produce the same result; it is just a little slower. Shipping a dog to the south and southwest from late spring on should be outlawed—or to the northern states in winter. Some airlines won't accept shipments when the temperatures at the destination are likely to be dangerous. They are right in doing that. A dog in a shipping crate is totally at the mercy of the elements and whoever is in charge. The dog can do nothing to help itself.

Bad baggage placement in the cargo or baggage compartment can suffocate a dog (and that has happened many times), and even if a dog is likely to be terrified by what is happening all around it, the use of tranquilizers is still not advisable. They interfere with the animal's ability to control its own body temperature. That is something to discuss with a veterinarian.

If you do ship your dog and you are on the same flight—and he isn't an under-the-seat-in-front-of-you breed—you usually can arrange with the airline to let you check on your friend at any intermediate stops your plane might make. If you are not on the same flight, you should make arrangements for the plane to be met at its destination and your dog properly taken care of by someone who understands dogs. The person should be waiting at the airport when the plane arrives. If you don't have friends near the destination who can do you this favor, check with a local humane society. They are always in need of funds and might take on the assignment in return for a donation. If that doesn't work, have your veterinarian check his list and give you the name of a local vet whose kennel help might provide an official greeter—for a price. Anything but sending your very good friend off into the wild blue yonder before all necessary provisions for his comfort and safety have been made. This is a very important issue. Dogs are killed every year because owners overlook the hazards it faces in an oven: an escape-proof box on an extremely hot day.

At least one airline I know of, American, has an "animals on board" check-off box on the preflight checklist. The pilot, copilot, and engineer all know fragile lives are at stake before they start the engines. That helps, or at least it can help.

The problem is that the airlines often do not charge

enough to carry animals and have to hire baggage handlers that are a pebble short of a beach. If it did cost more to ship your dog by air, if there were a special surcharge for animals in transit, shipping them would be safer. In our own case we never flew our animals—not once—we always used a well air-conditioned station wagon or van. The roof rack handled a large wire pen (broken down for shipping) that we could set up in the shade outside the wagon, in which our dogs could enjoy the passing parade. As the sun moved, so did the pen. The dogs were always secure, so we felt secure. The only problem was with our beloved, incredible Yankee, the giant Bloodhound. He was fine with other dogs passing by and doing a little sniffing near his turf—unless it was a Standard Poodle. Then Yankee would become so profoundly agitated and noisy that one of us had to go into the pen with him and get him to settle down. There was something about that "look" that really offended him. I don't know that he would have harmed another dog if he had the chance, but we decided not to find out. That's what it is like at the dog show. The exhibitors, judges, stewards, handlers—and the dogs as well—are all personalities unto themselves. They are expected to be.

Kids, Too

When the happy day comes and a dog is welcomed into the human family pack or circle, there should be something in the arrangement for everyone. In the case of show-quality dogs, for the younger human members, besides companionship and learning firsthand about responsibility, there is a highly competitive sport called Junior Showmanship. The competition is judged solely on the ability and skill of the juniors in handling their dogs, just as they would in the breed ring in a regular conformation show. Having a family interest or hobby in which kids can participate as well as adults is obviously an enormously healthy thing.

In this special competition the show qualities of the dog are not even to be considered, so say the rules. Certainly, however, a beautifully groomed dog with a solid show background and in excellent condition, including psychological motivation, is going to make the youngster who is showing it look a whole lot better than a combination of lesser elements. Kids who do go into Junior Showmanship and stay with it are likely to be involved with dogs as a lifelong enthusiasm. The best of the best, at least many of them, began this way. In the final analysis, it is a lot cheaper than booze, drugs, and psychiatry. How does it work?

The classes and divisions of junior showmanship are Novice, boys and girls who are at least ten years old and under eighteen on the day of the show who have not yet won three first-place awards; Open, same age group but the junior shall have won three first-place awards; Junior and Senior classes: when there is an age split into two divisions, ten to fourteen and over fourteen to eighteen. Best Junior Handler is a prize not always given, but if it is, the prize must be announced in the premium list in advance of the show.

The dogs in junior showmanship must be registered with the AKC and very often are retired show dogs with lots of savvy and plenty of spunk and energy left, making them still highly competitive. The dogs used by the kids can be entered for junior showmanship only or may also be showing in conformation or obedience at the same show. The dog must be owned by the participant or a member of the youngster's immediate family or household and be so registered.

The ribbons offered in the junior showmanship classes are: first, rose; second, brown; third, light green; fourth, gray; and if Best Junior Handler is offered, the ribbon is rose and green. The intensity and professionalism shown by the kids and the dogs in these competitions is remarkable and inspiring. They are both serious about the competition and deeply committed to the concept of winning. They are dog people with no reserves, and people dogs. They care. No quarterback, center, or shortstop was ever more serious. The ribbons are treasured possessions.

The purpose behind the dog show itself, as we have noted, is to select the best examples of each breed whose genes should be brought forward in a carefully planned breeding program. The purpose behind junior showmanship is no less precise. It is to assure the future of the sport and of fine dogs. To begin showing your dogs as an adult is just fine. On the other hand, if you come into it when you are ten or eleven years old, to be judged on your own skill and not the dog's degree of perfection, is an added dimension. Handlers, judges, breeders, exhibitors, experienced family members, are all anxious to help the juniors develop their skills. It is an important part of the wonderful world of dogs. In no small way it is the future of the whole grand affair.

The world of show-quality purebred dogs and their future is summed up for me in one image: I remember two kids, about fifteen, doing their homework together in the benching area. They were apparently good friends outside the show ring. Their dogs, one a Gordon Setter and the other a Cocker Spaniel, were lying on either side of them, heads on the appropriate lap. The kids were working away, apparently on their schoolwork, and petting their dogs at the same time. It was a pretty picture. Everything was in balance.

Parenthetically, the young participants in these competitions are usually delighted to learn one ruling the AKC passes down to all judges they will face: Under no circumstances should questions be used as a means of testing a junior's knowledge. It is one thing to memorize a sheet of wisdom and parrot it back and quite another to perform with your dog in front of a very critical audience. The only form of competition that I know of where you can win with words is a spelling bee. You can't take either an oral or a written exam to become MVP.

Details

Worth

Noting

Chapter

9

The Hound Group we outlined earlier in this book noted only one real Coonhound, the Black-and-Tan, that is recognized for conformation championship points under AKC regulations. It has been a registered breed with the AKC for years. It is one of many breeds descended from the far more ancient Bloodhound.

There are five other Coonhounds popular in the American South today that almost certainly will be registered by the AKC and shown in this country under their aegis eventually. One of them is the Plott Hound, which has already been approved and joined the Hound Group in the year 2000. Following the Plott Hound, someday, will be the Blue Tick Coonhound, American English Coonhound, Treeing Walker Coonhound, and Redbone Coonhound. As you explore the world of dogs, it is interesting to see how breeds emerge from cultures and then pass on their genes to more new breeds as they evolve. It has taken at least 150 to 200

AKC Titles

Earlier in this book we made a number of references to titles a dog can earn, especially when charting the remarkable career of Snickers the wonderdog.

We will compile here the complete list of AKC titles, noting which go before the dog's registered name and which after. It is rather like "Dr." and "M.D."

Titles before the Dog's Name

AFC—American Field Trial Champion
CH—Champion
DC—Dual Champion (CH and FC)
FC—Field Trial Champion (includes Lure Coursing)
HC—Herding Champion
OTCH—Obedience Trial Champion (includes the UD title)
CT—Tracking
TC—Triple Champion (CH, FC, and OTCH)

Titles after the Dog's Name

AX—Agility Excellent
CD—Companion Dog
CDX—Companion Dog Excellent
HI—Herding Intermediate
HS—Herding Started
HT—Herding Tested
HX—Herding Excellent
JC—Junior Courser
JE—Junior Earthdog

Titles after the Dog's Name (*cont.*)

JH—Junior Hunter
MX—Master Agility Excellent
MC—Master Courser
ME—Master Earthdog
MH—Master Hunter
NA—Novice Agility
OA—Open Agility
PT—Pretrial Tested
SC—Senior Courser
SE—Senior Earthdog
SH—Senior Hunter
TD—Tracking Dog
TDX—Tracking Dog Excellent
UD—Utility Dog
UDX—Utility Dog Excellent
VST—Variable Surface Tracker

I don't know of a dog that has earned anywhere near the whole bowl of alphabet soup. Indeed, I suspect that would be impossible to do given the life span of dogs and their high-performance span of a few brief years. For most people who start as novices to "show" their dog, Ch. is the goal and UDX is a wonderful second. That is a fine combination to retire with—beautiful by definition (Ch.) and bright as a rocket scientist (UDX)—and who could ask for anything more!

Roger A. Caras

centuries of the process to get us and the Coonhounds to where we are. It is about to happen.

As a matter of fact, as you explore the dog world, you will find discreet groups with at least some common ancestry, like the Coonhounds, that invite further exploration. As they wend their way through our history and aesthetics, you will see how the complexities are endless and the ramifications also beyond counting.

The matter of performance life span is of particular importance to people who really like large dogs. Our Bloodhounds fell into that category, and we are well aware of the heartbreak dog lovers must suffer. Every dog or cat we get is a tragedy waiting to happen to us eventually. In the case of the giants, it all comes to an end too soon.

Any dog of the Mastiff line is likely to be relatively short-lived. That includes (but not exclusively) the Great Dane, Newfoundland, Great Pyrenees, Saint Bernard, Bernese Mountain Dog, Mastiff, Bullmastiff, Bulldog, as well as the Bloodhound, Komondor, Borzoi, Irish Wolfhound, and Rottweiler. That Irish Wolfhound, for example, may not be fully mature until he is four or even five years old, but he may have pretty much lived out his life by the time he is seven or eight. For comparison, very much smaller dogs like the Schipperke and Pomeranian regularly live twelve to sixteen years or more. I have known of Schipperkes and Lhasa Apsos who passed their twentieth birthdays. A Jack Russell Terrier that we placed in a wonderful home (she had to have a wonderful home because she was born stone deaf and yet earned an obedience title) celebrated her nineteenth birthday before she began really going downhill.

Built-in Faults

There are, unfortunately, potential genetic faults in most breeds, and it can be somewhere between difficult and impossible to breed them out of a line. By choosing puppies from the best lines, it is sometimes possible to avoid trouble. There can be no guarantees, and as with any domestic animal, there is always the luck of the draw to contend with. Pick the healthiest-looking puppy from the healthiest-looking and -acting parents produced by the most honest, involved, and concerned fanciers and you can have the luck to come up with a fine companion and show dog. Do it any other way, puppy mill; pet shop; inexperienced, unthinking, and uncaring backyard breeder, and you will almost certainly come acropper.

There are huge differences in the frequency of potential faults in the different breeds, and that does point fingers of suspicion at many of today's breeders. You, as a potential owner, must choose very carefully. Faults include a great range of potential anguish for your dog—faults of the skeleton, hip displasia to shoulder dislocation; severe allergies; progressive retinal atrophy; hypoglycemia; diabetes; epilepsy—some breeds having as many as thirty or forty of them.

The Norwich and Norfolk Terriers have no recognized genetic faults, nor does the Harrier. The Great Pyrenees, on the other hand, has fifteen; the Great Dane sixteen, including epilepsy. The German Shorthaired Pointer has one potential fault listed, the tendency to form subcutaneous cysts; the Field Spaniel two; but the German Shepherd and the Labrador Retriever each have twenty-five. The Bulldog and the Cocker Spaniel lead the parade with thirty-nine and forty potential genetic faults, respectively.

The incidence of hip displasia isn't nearly as common in some breeds as in others. The Saint Bernard is the most frequently impacted of all breeds, while displasia is virtually unknown in some other breeds, such as the Saluki.

Genetic faults are a minefield where a potential owner should tread gingerly. Remember, a genetic fault is by definition a potentially inherited one. Learn as much as you can about the lines of the breed that attracts you the most. Don't do it the hard way. We did. We purchased a Bloodhound puppy only to have it pitch forward into its breakfast bowl dead of a heart attack at eight months of age. The breeder and her veterinarian both knew something we didn't know and we hadn't thought to ask. It was our fault; we should have inquired. Every puppy in that litter, as it turned out, had at least a heart murmur. Whoever's fault it is, losing an eight-month-old puppy is heartbreaking. It can be said that the puppy would have died anyway, when it did and how it did. It is just so much harder when the puppy is your own, one you have come to love. Guilt is built into these catastrophes. It is easy enough to handle guilt intellectually, but when it comes to the emotional elements, it is far more difficult.

The fact that a puppy has had genetic defects in its family background is no guarantee that they will recur in the generations of concern to you. On the other hand, however carefully you plan the breedings, those faults can pop up seemingly from nowhere. All you can do is the best you can, picking, matching, and perhaps praying. Raise your puppy with the help of your veterinarian using the best nutrition possible, make certain all of the shots are on time, and love your dog. It can go very well indeed. Just avoid those pet shops, puppy mills, and amateur backyard breeders. Give your puppy at least a level playing field and try to work with the breeders who are working with other fanciers of your breed and veterinary research facilities to eliminate genetic faults and improve the strength and vigor of what is by this time "your breed."

Afterword

There, then, we have the basics. If you want to show a
dog and become a part of the sport you have admired,
these are the things you will have to know to start. It is not
space physics and not brain surgery, but it is an exercise in
knowing and caring. It is the ability to give and to get.

First you have to have a dog not only suitable to the task
but as taken with the whole idea as you are. There are to be
two of you out there on display and you both have to have
the same thing in mind, winning. Most exhibitors are at
least marginally smarter than their dogs, so it is natural for
them to lead the way. The dogs will go along with that.

Once you have taken the biggest and most important
steps of all and chosen your breed and then, clearly step
number two, chosen your individual dog, the training begins. When you are in that phase you have a clear shot for
the peak. Don't stop and don't look back. Just get better and
better at the game and help your dog hold up his end. Win

167

and then win again. After your winner has a Ch. in front of his name, you may want to think about breeding him or her to the best partner you can find. Explore other aspects of the dog sport, such as obedience, agility, and the others we have discussed. You will have met any number of people by that time who have the same kind of interest in the same breed you do. Talk things over. Presumably you didn't stint in choosing your dog. Try not to stint in choosing a mate for it. Your skill as a matchmaker has a great deal to do with how the puppies turn out.

One other point: About sixty-three days after the breeding, the puppies will appear. If you have not had experience in the whelping process you may want to have someone on hand to help you who has had experience—a breeder, a veterinarian, or a vet tech. Give your puppies every chance there is for a good life, and that starts with a good beginning. Talk it over with your veterinarian. Get the details right. Everything from a heat lamp to the whelping box itself should be perfect.

Going back a step, you will notice something strange happening with your feelings about your original puppy. When you two first meet you will want to hug him—he is cute, after all! Puppies are supposed to be cute and huggable. His eyes look straight ahead, just as your eyes do. He makes heartwarming squealing sounds and reacts with his whole body when you tickle him. He will have puppy breath, which is practically an aphrodisiac for dog lovers, and he will squiggle and you will squeeze. Something wonderful is beginning to happen. It is a string of markedly fuzzy moments, and you may be surprised to see how susceptible to fuzzy moments you are. The process is called revelation. You are probably a pushover.

But then, day by day, the change will progress. It will grow and grow and grow. Your reaction to fuzzy will mature into a solid relationship. When your dog looks up at you (a typical man-dog spatial relationship, since our heads are on top of us and the dogs' are out front of them pointing to wherever it is they are going), there will be eye contact, and then you will realize the miracle that has occurred—you really do understand each other. And you certainly are profoundly interested in each other. You care about each other. You have bonded and now you are friends in a way peculiar to just the two of you. There is pride in this and some nervousness, of course, because the showing is about to begin. Fortunately, you are able to relieve each other's tensions. You touch. But typically the other comes first: first you love your dog and then you put him to the test, and then finally you begin to collect and display his trophies and ribbons. You do all this together, the two of you. By now you will be boasting. The circle is closing and you and your dog are inside it. Enjoy.